WHAT WAS I THINKING?

THINGS I'VE LEARNED

SINCE I KNEW IT ALL

HOWARD BOOKS
An Imprint of Simon & Schuster, Inc.

NEW YORK   NASHVILLE   LONDON   TORONTO   SYDNEY   NEW DELHI

STEVE BROWN

To my beloved friend and mentor,

FRED SMITH,

whose life has so deeply affected mine

and whose wisdom and teaching are

such an important (albeit unspoken)

part of this book.

Howard Books
An Imprint of Simon & Schuste, Inc.
1230 Avenue of the Americas
New York, NY 10020

First Howard Books trade paperback edition December 2015

HOWARD and colophon are trademarks of Simon & Schuster, Inc.

For information about special discounts for bulk purchases, please contact Simon & Schuster Special Sales at 1-800-506-1949 or business@simonandschuster.com.

The Simon & Schuster Speakers Bureau can bring authors to your live event. For more information or to book and event contact the Simon & Schuster Speakers Bureau at 1-866-248-3049 or visit our website at www.simonspeakers.com.

Interior design by John Mark Luke Designs

Manufactured in the United States of America

10 9 8 7 6 5 4 3 2 1

Library of Congress Cataloging-in-Publication Data is available.

ISBN 978-1-58229-570-1
ISBN 978-1-5011-3205-6 (pbk)
ISBN 978-1-4165-4252-0 (ebook)

CONTENTS

ACKNOWLEDGMENTS
vii

INTRODUCTION:
WHAT WAS I THINKING?
1

CHAPTER 1:
GOD IS A LOT BIGGER THAN I THOUGHT HE WAS
5

CHAPTER 2:
JESUS IS A LOT MORE RADICAL THAN I THOUGHT HE WAS
25

CHAPTER 3:
THE HOLY SPIRIT IS WORKING IN A LOT MORE PLACES
THAN I THOUGHT HE WAS
43

CHAPTER 4:
THE BIBLE REVEALS A LOT MORE THAN I THOUGHT IT DID
63

CHAPTER 5:
THE BATTLE IS A LOT MORE SUPERNATURAL THAN I THOUGHT IT WAS
79

CHAPTER 6:
PEOPLE ARE A LOT WORSE THAN I THOUGHT THEY WERE
93

Contents

CHAPTER 7:

People Are a Lot Better Than I Thought They Were

111

CHAPTER 8:

Self-Righteousness Is a Lot More Dangerous
Than I Thought It Was

129

CHAPTER 9:

Obedience Is a Lot More Difficult
Than I Thought It Was

147

CHAPTER 10:

Love Is a Lot Stronger Than I Thought It Was

165

CHAPTER 11:

The World Is a Lot More Dangerous
Than I Thought It Was

181

CHAPTER 12:

Things Will Work Out a Lot Better
Than I Thought They Would

199

NOTES:

215

ACKNOWLEDGMENTS

THE DANGER IN thanking people who make a book possible is in leaving out the names of significant people who made this book possible or, on the other hand, including names of significant people who don't want to be associated with it.

Nevertheless, I must mention my wife, who makes all that I do better and continues to love me when it isn't.

And I must not forget . . .

Denny and Philis Boultinghouse, at Howard Books, who struggle to make me write and then make it better when I do.

Dawn Brandon and Tammy Bicket, whose skilled editing fixed what I wrote and possibly kept me out of jail.

My friends, the staff at Key Life, who continue to "hold up my arms" and do stuff for which I get the credit.

My friends and colleagues at Reformed Theological Seminary in Orlando, who struggle to keep me from being a heretic.

My friend Tom Wood, who found a quote that only he and God knew.

And finally, Robin DeMurga, through whose skilled writing and editing hands passes everything I write here and a thousand other places.

If you're on the list and didn't want to be . . . deal with it!

What Was I Thinking?

One time Mark Twain's wife got furious with him and did something she rarely, if ever, did. She started cursing. Twain started laughing, and that, of course, made her even angrier. She asked him what he thought was so funny.

"My dear," he said through gales of laughter, "you know the words, but you don't know the tune!"

Some things should be settled in a believer's life. The eternal verities of the faith should not be adjusted to fit the times, softened to fit the culture, or set aside to fit the changing whims of modern proclivities. Truth is truth because it is true, and it is true in every place and at every time. Real truth doesn't change.

There was a time when I thought that knowing the truth was enough. I defended it (still do), taught it (still do), and believed that if you got the truth right, everything else would be right.

I'm a lot older now, and some wiser. I was wrong. I got the words right, but I missed the tune.

This book is about the tune.

A number of years ago, a friend of mine left the denomination of which I'm a part. The doctrinal basis of my denomination is a confession of faith, the Westminster Confession of Faith, which contains many of the doctrines of the Reformation.

In our conversation, I asked my friend if he still believed that the Confession was true.

"Of course it's true," he replied. "It's just irrelevant."

Before we begin, let me state for the record that my theology is orthodox, evangelical, and Reformed. By that I mean that I believe the historic creeds of the Christian faith, I accept the Westminster Confession of Faith as representing the basic doctrines of the Christian faith, and I believe the Bible is true—all of it. Not only that. I believe that the Bible, the creeds, and the Confession are vitally important. They are important like the foundation of a building. They are like the words of a song.

I tell you this for two reasons. First, some of what I'm going to say in this book will make you wonder about my orthodox credentials. And second, I believe the very thing that points one to Christ (i.e., the foundational biblical truths) can also become death to us if, once we go to Christ, we stop there—in other words, if we then get a polemical gun and see our call from God as defending the orthodoxy that got us there.

I've been there, done that, have the T-shirt . . . and it almost killed me. Theology (no matter how orthodox), a belief statement (no matter how biblical), and propositions (no matter how exact and correct) are all useless if they don't lead us to the reality which is God and to the astonishment that ought to be a regular occurrence in the believer's life.

Of late I've looked at the words—those statements of faith—that I thought were enough and have come to the sobering realization that if we get the words right but can't sing the tune, we miss the grandeur of the song. I've looked at my years of ministry and teaching; I've read old sermons I've preached and books I've written; I've thought of the people with whom I've worked and of the battles I've fought.

As I've revisited those places, I haven't been ashamed of the truth, but I have often said to myself, "What in the world was I thinking?"

This is a book written by an old guy who started out with the right words but has spent most of his life learning the tune. Along the way I've discovered that the Christian faith is far more radical and far less cerebral than I thought it was.

I would really like to go back and re-teach some of the things I've taught to the congregations I've served and at the conferences and seminars where I've spoken. I don't want to re-teach the words of the song. I got those right. I want to teach—as the song says—the world to sing.

Of course, I can't do that. I don't have that kind of time, and I'm not sure people would understand.

So I'm writing this book instead.

I don't know about you, but I'm tired of glib answers to hard questions, irrelevant "God words," and stark, cold foundations on which no house has ever been built. This book is not about the foundations (i.e., the words). If you're still struggling with the truth of the Christian faith, read another book.

In this book are my second thoughts on matters of first importance, with the hope of putting music to the words.

So, can you carry a tune?

A VOICE IN THE WIND I DO NOT KNOW;
A MEANING ON THE FACE OF THE HIGH HILLS
WHOSE UTTERANCE I CANNOT COMPREHEND,
A SOMETHING IS BEHIND THEM: THAT IS GOD.

George MacDonald

GOD IS A LOT BIGGER THAN I THOUGHT HE WAS

From him and through him and to him are all things.
To him be glory forever. Amen.

ROMANS 11:36

TRUTH IS TRUTH—unchangeable and eternal. That is especially true with God. As I mentioned in the introduction, theology (no matter how orthodox), a belief statement (no matter how biblical), and propositions (no matter how exact and correct) are all useless unless they lead to the reality of God himself.

I started out with all the right words yet somehow missed the tune. I hadn't gone far enough.

What was I thinking? Perhaps I was thinking too much. Let me say it again: the Christian faith is far more radical and far less cerebral than I thought it was.

Sometimes I wish I knew as much as my students. There was a time when I thought I did.

It's said that the late Albert Schweitzer—the German theologian, musicologist, philosopher, and missionary (a Nobel laureate)—was working on a construction project, building a hospital. One of the nationals came by, and Schweitzer asked him to help. The young man refused on the grounds that he was an intellectual.

5

"I thought," Schweitzer said, turning back to his work, "that I was an intellectual once."

I thought I was one too.

I struggled for years with the eternal verities of the Christian faith. I had an undergraduate degree with a major in philosophy and religion, and I was working through some really hard stuff. I read more books than many people will ever read, asked more questions than many will ever ask, and pushed my epistemological presuppositions to the wall. After the struggle, I came to the Christian worldview from which I now live.

I thought I was at the end of my theological journey. Once the foundations were settled, I thought it was all settled.

I didn't know it then, but it wasn't settled at all.

There is no "settled" when it comes to God. For me, faith was cerebral. And having a relationship with God—the real God—is so much more than that. What *was* I thinking?

I often say to my students, when they are especially strident about a subject, "You haven't lived long enough, sinned big enough, or failed nearly enough to even have an opinion on that."

Well, I have lived long enough, sinned big enough, and failed enough. So I want to share with you what I know about God—which, frankly, isn't as much as I once thought it was.

A BIG GOD

An acquaintance of mine has two earned doctorates. During his academic work, he was an atheist; but as he approached his final dissertation, he had a number of important questions. "The first question on my list," he said, "is this: is there a God? If there is a God, then he's in charge. If there isn't a God, then I'm in charge."

Good point, that.

It is not the main point, however. The main point is what we come to through this line of questioning: If there is a God, and he is in charge, what does it mean? Where will it lead? What are the implications of that fact? Does it really matter? Given that he is infinite and I'm finite, does it even matter that he's in charge? Why should I—a mere mortal—care who is in charge? It may be fate, a system, or God, but someone else is in control, so it's all the same. God is in his heaven, and I am here on earth. There are matters, appropriately, about which I can do nothing, for which I have no plan, and on which I have no vote.

A friend of mine drew a cartoon of two ants standing next to the leg of an elephant. One ant says to the other ant, "Let me introduce you to my new friend. I really didn't want to be his friend, but when something that big insists, it is a good policy not to offer any resistance."

Back to our questions. If God is the elephant, what's an ant to do? Frankly, not much. Then again, a whole lot . . . we'll get to that later in this chapter and throughout the book.

The wise preacher who wrote the book of Ecclesiastes said this:

> I turned about and gave my heart up to despair over all the toil of my labors under the sun, because sometimes a person who has toiled with wisdom and knowledge and skill must leave everything to be enjoyed by someone who did not toil for it. This also is vanity and a great evil. What has a man from all the toil and striving of heart with which he toils beneath the sun? For all his days are full of sorrow, and his work is a

vexation. Even in the night his heart does not rest. This also is vanity. (2:20–23)

For those of you who think the Bible is an unrealistic book, put that in your pipe and smoke it. That, of course, isn't all the Bible says. But a good place to start is with this understanding of God's absolute sovereignty. We don't get a vote.

THE REAL GOD

I used to think I had God figured out. I put him into my theological box, nice and tidy. Now I realize that God simply doesn't fit in that box. God is not who I thought he was.

A business friend of mine is very good at what he does. In fact, Sam is quite rich, and he's rich because he's better at what he does than his competitors are. Before I knew my friend, I knew some of his competitors. One day, for some reason known only to himself, and before Sam was even an acquaintance, he invited me to lunch. Some of his competitors heard about the appointment and issued warnings: "He would sell his mother if he could make a buck," one told me. "You don't even want to be seen in a restaurant with that man. It will hurt your reputation," another said. "If I were you, I would turn down the invitation. There's no such thing as a free lunch," another advised.

Against this advice, I accepted the lunch invitation and, in fact, ended up having lunch with Sam on a fairly regular basis. We became friends. It worked because I didn't want anything from him, and he didn't want anything from me. We were both just looking for a friend. I quickly learned that Sam wasn't anything like what I'd been told about him.

As I've gotten older, I've discovered that God isn't altogether what I thought he was either. Some people have been misrepresenting him too. Don't get me wrong; these people don't know they're misrepresenting him. In fact, they think they're doing God and others a great service. Nonetheless, perhaps their perceptions don't get to the heart of who God is. So I want to, as it were, invite you to have lunch with him.

You might be surprised.

Perhaps people have told you that God is a "child abuser"—a Father who will cut off our legs if we get out of line. Or that he is eternally disappointed with us and that his disappointment was reflected in the cross. Perhaps they said there are certain people God loves and certain people he doesn't love. He has been portrayed in books, on broadcasts, and from pulpits as a religious God who wants everybody to be religious—or else. And then there were others who told us God is sort of like Santa who gives gifts, like a favorite uncle who affirmed and loved us, or like a grandfather who stayed up at night admiring us.

> AS I'VE GOTTEN OLDER, I'VE DISCOVERED THAT GOD ISN'T ALTOGETHER WHAT I THOUGHT HE WAS.

I did my fair share of misrepresenting God. I was quite secure in my worldview—I believed it, taught it, defended it, and wrote about it.

Then God—the God of the universe, the real God—came . . . and put me in my place.

A Scary God

If you've never stood before God and been afraid, then you've probably never stood before the real God. (It doesn't end there—

with fear—but that is where it starts.) I used to think that God was nice and safe. Now I know that he is scary.

As long as I could keep God in church, in my theology books, and in my academic discussions, I could deal with him. But when the real God came, it felt like he shook the church, burned the books, and laughed at my academic discussions. I then realized that one doesn't "deal with" God. He deals with us.

The church where I'm a member is a bit different from most. Do you know what our elders gave my pastor for his birthday? They gave him a forty-five. Yeah, a gun. Don't ask me. Maybe it was for church discipline or something—be holy as God is holy . . . or our pastor will shoot you dead.

I have a book in my library titled *Bible in Pocket, Gun in Hand*. It's about the early circuit riders in America. Maybe our elders were reverting to an earlier and simpler time when things were clear: do it our way or pay the consequences.

Well, God doesn't wield a gun. But he isn't "safe" either.

The book of Job is a philosophical discussion about the problems of suffering, evil, and pain. These problems are debated in college dorm rooms everywhere; nobody has any answers, but it's fun to talk about the questions. The difference between the book of Job and a dorm-room debate is that with Job, the questions weren't just theory. His questions were of great existential importance because he was not an outsider talking about the philosophical problem of suffering. Job had lost his family, his possessions, his reputation, and his friends. He sat on an ash heap, scraping the scabs off his sores, and he had had it.

Don't let people use Job as an example of an especially spiritual person who took his suffering the way Christians are supposed to take it: praising God. He did that, but only once. He said, "Though he slay me, I will hope in him" (13:15). After that, Job reverted to a normal human reaction—anger, bitterness, and self-pity. He was ticked, and he yelled at God.

When Job had told God what he really thought, God asked, essentially, "Are you finished?"

Then God started asking some very intimidating questions. Job, having encountered the real God, had an attack of sanity and said, "I had heard of you by the hearing of the ear, but now my eye sees you; therefore I despise myself, and repent in dust and ashes" (42:5–6).

God is scary . . . really scary. So be afraid . . . be very afraid.

Why do you think the Scriptures say no one has ever seen the face of God? Why do you think prophets hid their faces from God? Why do you think Elijah ran and Jeremiah wept? Why do you think Jacob almost died wrestling with an angel? Why do you think Paul said he was talking like a fool when he bragged? Why do you think most folks don't read the book of Revelation or, if they do, feel the need to soften it?

Because one does not trifle with a God who is big and scary.

In my saner moments I'm glad he's that way. Little gods do little things. They speak silly words, and while they might be less threatening, little gods don't give us meaning, demand anything of us, or inspire us.

A GOD IN CONTROL

I used to think (or at least hope) that I was the one in control. Now I know that God is the only one in control. I'm not. I'm helpless.

I'm big into control. I'm an adult child of an alcoholic, and that means I have the perception that every time I've been out of control, I've gotten hurt. So I try to control everything in my life. My theology is an effort to get some kind of handle on God and control him. My religious profession is, I suppose, an effort to control God too. I pray and preach and teach about God to get some kind of handle on him.

This is slowly beginning to change for me. Over the years I've begun to loosen my grip. To be honest, I didn't have any choice in the matter. When you encounter the real God, you learn that he simply refuses to be controlled.

That was Paul's experience. In his letter to the Romans, Paul sounds like a helpless man—because that's exactly what he was. He wrote, "I do not understand my own actions. For I do not do what I want, but I do the very thing I hate. . . . Wretched man that I am! Who will deliver me from this body of death?" (Romans 7:15–24).

The psalmist cried out to God, "O LORD, God of my salvation; I cry out day and night before you. . . . Incline your ear to my cry! For my soul is full of troubles, and my life draws near to Sheol. . . . Your wrath lies heavy upon me, and you overwhelm me with all your waves" (Psalm 88:1–7).

If you've ever had kidney stones, what I'm going to say next won't surprise you.

YIKES!

I have women friends who've had both kidney stones and babies, and they actually say that the pain of having a kidney stone is worse than the pain of childbirth because at least when delivering a baby, you get a baby. With a kidney stone, all you get is that stupid stone.

At any rate, when I went through my experience with kidney stones, at first I didn't know what it was and thought I was going to die. As my wife took me to the hospital, I was thinking about my will. Who would get my computer? Was my insurance up to date? Whom would my wife marry after I was gone?

When I got to the hospital, they gave me a shot, and I felt wonderful. Then they gave me pills, and whenever the pain got bad, I just popped a pill. Then a surgeon—who seemed to me a very young surgeon, kind of like Doogie Howser—explained what he was going to do about getting the stone out. I said something like, "Oh no, you're not! I can live on these happy pills the rest of my life."

But I didn't have any choice. After a while the pills would begin to lose their potency. I could cuss and spit, but that wouldn't help get rid of the stone. In fact, there wasn't a thing I could do but go through with the surgery. So do you know what I did? I let go. I couldn't fix the problem, and I couldn't make the situation any better. All I could do was take the anesthetic, go to sleep, and let the surgeon do his work.

> WHEN YOU ENCOUNTER THE REAL GOD, YOU LEARN THAT HE SIMPLY REFUSES TO BE CONTROLLED.

When the real God comes to us, he is like the surgeon. He is going to do what he is going to do, and I'm helpless to change or fix anything. I don't get a vote, and it drives me nuts. Not only that. I'm powerless to get him to stop because, as C. S. Lewis said, God is a *good* surgeon. He won't stop until he accomplishes whatever he has determined to accomplish.

I feel completely helpless.

That is appropriate.

I am.

I used to say that God and I were partners. We're not. He is God, and I am not. So sometimes the most important thing I can do is get out of the way.

A CONFUSING GOD

I used to think that I had God down. Now I realize that much of the time, all I am is confused.

Does God confuse you? Have you ever been sure that God told you to do something or promised something only to find out that you were wrong—terribly wrong? Have you ever pontificated about God only to find out that you didn't speak from Sinai, and you had to eat crow? Have you ever told someone that God told you to tell that person something and then found out that the person got into serious trouble because of your dumb remarks? Have you ever thought that you had seen God, only to find out that you were crazy? Have you ever answered questions about God not because you knew the answers but because you simply had a glib tongue or were trying to cover for your lack of answers?

I have.

In Romans 11:34 Paul asked a rhetorical question: "Who has known the mind of the Lord, or who has been his counselor?" The answer to that question is, of course, nobody. No one has understood God, and no one has ever helped him out with advice. "For my thoughts are not your thoughts, neither are your ways my ways, declares the LORD. For as the heavens are higher than the earth, so are my ways higher than your ways and my thoughts than your thoughts" (Isaiah 55:8–9).

I teach through a syndicated radio broadcast called *Key Life.* On part of Wednesday's program and on all of Friday's program (when my pastor, Pete Alwinson, joins me), I devote time to answering some of the thousands of questions we receive at Key Life Network. In addition, at almost all of the conferences and seminars this ministry conducts around the country, we include a segment during which I answer questions. I also spend considerable time at Reformed Theological Seminary answering questions from students.

I used to be anxious about those Q&A sessions. No more. I'm no longer anxious because I generally know more than those who are asking the questions. That isn't pride; it's just true. After all, I've been at this longer than most of them. (Would you go to a surgeon who doesn't know more than you do about surgery?)

More importantly, though, I'm comfortable with those Q&A sessions because I don't mind responding, "I don't know. I don't have the foggiest idea about how to answer your question, and I am, as a matter of fact, probably more confused than you are."

Do you remember the Y2K scare, when the "experts" predicted that all of civilization would come to a screeching halt because computers were programmed to work with two-digit numbers for years, like 98 or 99, and wouldn't be able to transition to using four digits, like 2000 or 2001?

I didn't buy into the mania. So when the great crash didn't happen, boy did I have fun on my next broadcast.

I love making fun of "experts" who are wrong. There is so much arrogance, so much self-righteousness, and so much self-aggrandizement in many experts that when they're wrong (and they often are), it's hard to resist pointing it out.

God does that to us sometimes, when we're acting like experts: "Who is this that darkens counsel by words without knowledge? Dress for action like a man; I will question you, and you make it known to me" (Job 38:2–3). In other words, what do we know about his plans or his ways? If we're honest, very little.

A few months ago I was the officiating minister at the funeral of a teenage boy who had committed suicide. I guess people expected me to explain how a good God could allow such a tragedy.

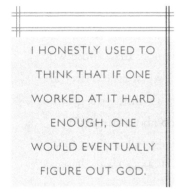

I HONESTLY USED TO THINK THAT IF ONE WORKED AT IT HARD ENOUGH, ONE WOULD EVENTUALLY FIGURE OUT GOD.

There was a time when I would have tried. But instead, I said, "I don't understand this. It makes me angry and confused. So if you're angry and confused, at least we can cry together."

Angry and confused. I'm not sure about the anger, but I do believe confusion is appropriate when standing before the real God.

I honestly used to think that if one worked at it hard enough, studied the Bible long enough, and talked to the right people often enough, one would eventually figure out God. I'm an old guy now, and I've been doing all three for a long time. And I was wrong.

GOD'S WEIRD CHOICES

I used to think that God liked only certain people—those who lived up to his standards. But I'm increasingly surprised by his choice of friends. And even more surprised that his choice includes me.

God makes what seem to me some very funny choices—

meaning, they're not necessarily the choices I would make. You see, I always thought God had a big house in which the people who did what he said could live, worship, and enjoy fellowship. On the outside were the people who didn't do what God said to do. I, of course, was on the inside, because I did what he said— or at least tried to. I figured my sincerity would give me a pass.

But I was wrong.

God said to Moses in Exodus 33:19, "I will make all my goodness pass before you and will proclaim before you my name 'The LORD.' And I will be gracious to whom I will be gracious, and will show mercy on whom I will show mercy." In other words, God will choose his own friends, thank you very much.

That has always bothered me.

I am probably as religious as any person you know. Maybe even more. I teach religion to religious students at a religious graduate school. I stand before a whole lot of people and say religious things. I write religious books, I teach religious seminars, and I do religious radio broadcasts.

I'm really religious.

What bugs me is when God chooses to love people who aren't religious or, at any rate, not as religious as I am. I'm beginning to learn that God makes, by my judgment, some weird choices. He loves people who drive me nuts, and he has mercy on people to whom I would not show mercy. He moves beyond religious institutions and befriends people with whom I would not be friends.

Whoopi Goldberg, who calls herself an atheist, is not one of my favorite people. But did you see her movie *Sister Act*? It's about a prostitute who hides from some thugs who want to kill her. What makes it unique is that she hides in a Roman Catholic convent. She dresses like a nun and becomes the choir director, teaching the nuns to sing music that's more upbeat and fun than their usual convent fare.

OK, that's cool and a good story.

But what makes the story for me is this: Early in the film, the convent church is old and filled with old people who are very religious. Once the prostitute/nun starts leading the choir, however, the people on the outside (prostitutes, drug addicts, and other colorful characters) start coming into the church. In fact, they fill the church.

When I first saw that scene, I started crying. (I hardly cry at anything. I'm a guy, OK?) My wife, who was with me, gave me a look that said clearly, "Will you stop it? Are you a fruitcake? This is a comedy. Can't you see that everybody else in this theater is laughing, and you're crying? I think I'm going to sit somewhere else and pretend that I don't know you."

Nevertheless, I couldn't stop weeping. When the movie was over, I asked God about my peculiar reaction, and I felt him answer that it wasn't me—it was him. He was speaking through that scene.

I whined in response. *But Lord, Whoopi Goldberg? Why couldn't it have been through Billy Graham or the Pope?*

I didn't get an answer.

I have a recurring dream in which I'm finally home in heaven and am sitting at the Lord's table for the marriage supper of the Lamb. All kinds of people are there: those who were once homosexuals, pornographers, and gluttons. As I look around, I also see former adulterers, liars, and thieves. There are one-time prostitutes and pimps, tax collectors and drunks. I'm generally pleased that some clergy persons are present, some leaders of the church, and even one or two television preachers. And, frankly, I'm shocked.

Then, in my dream, I hear a voice from the throne, and the words are addressed to me. The voice is God's, and he asks, "And what do you think you're doing here?"

I think maybe he was kidding, but I'm not sure. I usually wake up before I find out.

A Loving God

I used to think God's love could be logically explained and measured. I now know that God's love runs far deeper than we can fathom.

There was a time when I was sure I could explain and defend God. I've found out, though, that he is beyond explanation—and not in need of defense. He was doing fine before I came along, and he will do fine long after I'm gone. Yet for some reason, this big, scary, and confusing God who chooses unlikely friends has chosen to love me. And I see his love in everything, without exception. The question is not, "Where is God's love?" The question is, "Where *isn't* God's love?"

Frankly, the love thing makes me even more confused about God. I could understand a monster God, a God who was justly angry at his creatures who have messed things up so terribly—or even a God who was on vacation. But a God who loves people who don't deserve love?

It's true. "God so loved the world, that he gave his only Son" (John 3:16).

Charles Spurgeon said that if we can't trace God's hand, we should trust his heart. I feel like I've been doing a lot of heart-trusting as of late. Every time I have a question about God (and I have a lot), every time I'm confused (and I'm confused a lot), and every time I feel helpless (and I feel helpless a lot), I have to trust God's heart. Because I can't trace his hand.

Brian McLaren has written, among other books, three semi-fictional works about "Pastor Dan" and his postmodern friend and mentor. The third book is titled *The Last Word and the Word after That: A Tale of Faith, Doubt, and a New Kind of Christianity.* While I don't agree with everything Dr. McLaren wrote, I am in agreement with his belief that our real problem in the church is that we start with the doctrine of hell rather than with the doctrine of God's character.

What is God like? That's the first question. How we answer it—how we understand God's character—determines how we deal with all other questions. I'm confused about a lot of stuff, but if I begin at one truth that is clearly taught in Scripture, demonstrated in the incarnation of Christ, and experienced in my own life—that God isn't just loving, and he doesn't just act in loving ways, but he *is* love (see 1 John 4:16)—then it helps me put everything else into proper perspective.

Perhaps you've heard the song that says, "God is good. He is good all the time." Well, he is. I don't know if I fully understand that. I have a lot of questions about it. But the bottom line is, God's is the heart I trust. And trusting his heart of love, I've discovered a supernatural peace and meaning that could not have come from my questions.

After Jesus's resurrection, he appeared on the shore of the Sea of Tiberias and fixed breakfast for his astonished disciples. During that encounter (see John 21), Jesus asked Peter if Peter loved him—and he asked Peter that same question three times. I suppose Jesus was giving Peter the opportunity to speak his love three times, once for each earlier betrayal.

It was a good question.

My question, in the face of uncertainties, fear, helplessness, and confusion, is the same as Jesus's question—only reversed. "Jesus, are you sure you love us? Sometimes it seems you don't treat your friends very well, and we wonder. Are you there? Do you care? Are you angry?"

And then, very hesitantly, "Do you . . . uh . . . love me?"

The answer is always a clear yes, and I find it throughout the Bible and throughout my life. I've gotten the answer in the way I've been forgiven. I've experienced God's love in the laughter of my grandchildren and in the beauty of a sunset. I've seen it in the tears of a friend who was weeping over my sin and in the sermon by which my pastor reminded me that God had not gone away on vaca-

GOD ISN'T JUST LOVING, AND HE DOESN'T JUST ACT IN LOVING WAYS, BUT HE *IS* LOVE.

tion. I've seen God's love for me in the church, made up of imperfect people who have stopped playing games, and in books that helped me know his truth and grace.

But I've also experienced God's love when I've seen Jesus in the faces of devastated families who've lost a child. I've met God and experienced his love by the bedsides of people who are dying of cancer, and I've seen it in the eyes of people who have tried and failed over and over again.

And always God's tears mingle with ours. I know because I know him in his tears and in his love. God *is* love.

I used to think that understanding him was the main thing. It isn't. The main thing is being loved by him. And that I know.

IS IT ANY WONDER THAT TO THIS DAY THIS GALILEAN

IS TOO MUCH FOR OUR SMALL HEARTS?

H. G. WELLS

JESUS IS A LOT MORE RADICAL THAN I THOUGHT HE WAS

The law was given through Moses; grace and truth came through Jesus Christ. No one has ever seen God; the only God, who is at the Father's side, he has made him known.

JOHN 1:17–18

I HAVE A confession to make: I've had to change what I thought about Jesus.

Perhaps the most salient fact about Jesus is that he surprises us. Well, *surprise* may not be the right word. He offends, amazes, shocks, and confuses us. And he refuses to fit into the mold we've designed for him.

And Jesus surprised—and offended, amazed, shocked, and confused—me.

Did you hear about the man who was given a tour of the various levels of hell? The first level was horrible, and he asked his tour guide what the people held there had done. The guide said, "Those are Baptists who danced."

The second level of hell was even worse. To the man's query, the guide responded, "These were the Episcopalians who spent their capital."

When they got to the third level, it was a lot worse. The man asked the tour director what those people had done. "They're Pentecostals who refused to raise their hands," he replied.

Finally they reached the deepest level of hell. The people there were in utter agony. "Good heavens," the man said. "What did these people do?"

"They're Presbyterians," said the tour director, "who smiled, said, 'Praise the Lord!' in a formal worship service, and used the wrong fork at dinner."

That joke wasn't funny to me for the longest time. Do you know why?

I had made Jesus into a Presbyterian! Is that crazy or what?

Don't get me wrong . . . I thought he should be. In fact, for years I tried to force him into that mold—nice, proper, and if he had lived in the twenty-first century, an owner of blue-chip stocks. I always thought Jesus would be comfortable in most Presbyterian churches and would subscribe to the Westminster Confession of Faith. If his incarnation had taken place in modern times, I was quite certain he would be a Republican.

What was I thinking?

All that was before I understood the real Jesus. He didn't frighten me as much as God the Father did, but he did confuse me.

Jesus simply doesn't fit into our mold. If Jesus were just a man, that wouldn't be a big deal. It's not so surprising when people do weird things. I can deal with a psychotic megalomaniac or, perhaps, a neurotic religious nut. But when Jesus offends, amazes, shocks, and confuses us, that's another matter altogether, because he isn't just a man. He's God.

Jesus actually claimed godhood. That would be sick if not

for the evidence of crutches thrown jubilantly into the air and of empty caskets. At the reports of a dead man getting up and walking around, I decided I should listen to what was said by the one who had raised him.

And that man said he is God.

In chapter one I made reference to Albert Schweitzer. He's a hero to me not so much because of what he did but because of what he wrote. In fact, if Schweitzer had never written anything but what follows, taken from his book *The Quest of the Historical Jesus*, it would be enough:

> He [Jesus] comes to us as One unknown, without a name, as of old, by the lake side, He came to those men who knew Him not. He speaks to us the same word, "Follow thou me!" and sets us to the tasks which He has to fulfill for our time. He commands. And to those who obey Him, whether they be wise or simple, He will reveal Himself in the toils, the conflicts, the sufferings which they shall pass through in His fellowship, and as an ineffable mystery, they shall learn in their own experience Who He is.[1]

If you want evidence of the truth in Schweitzer's words, I'm it.

It's not that I've always obeyed Jesus, but I've followed him for a long time, and I'm still here. I'm bloodied, sinful, and afraid . . . but I'm still here. The longer I follow Jesus, the more I learn about him—and the more I've had to change what I think about him.

Jesus as God

The problem was, I had made Jesus into a doctrine, and while there are important truths *about* him, those facts aren't who he is.

Most Christians, myself included, have quite rightly looked at the incarnation of God in Christ as foundational to the theological superstructure of our faith. It's one of those "but of course" doctrines we've simply accepted. But perhaps we accepted it too quickly.

Did you know that almost all Christian heresies, as defined by the church, are Christological heresies? In other words, the central place where people get it wrong, according to the historic church councils, is in the definition of who Jesus is and what he did.

I can understand that.

The incarnation of God in Christ is a crazy doctrine. If you don't find it difficult to believe or, if you do believe it, to apply, then you simply haven't understood how radical the coming of Jesus was. Much of my life, I've tried to make the incarnation of Christ palatable to the rational minds of the people to whom I believe God has sent me. I've softened it, repackaged it, and even tried to redefine it. The reason is this: I knew that if I were not a believer, this is the place where I would stumble.

> THE DOCTRINE OF THE INCARNATION OF GOD IN CHRIST IS THE "EATING A FROG," AS IT WERE, ASPECT OF THE CHRISTIAN WORLDVIEW.

If I weren't a Christian and you were, I would understand your beliefs about God's existence (only a fool, the Bible says, subscribes to atheism), immortality (I'm not really that happy about dying and could use a little hope), and ethics (they keep stealing my car, and somebody has to say that's wrong). If I weren't a Christian, I would probably even have a secret hope that you were right.

But when you started talking about Jesus being God, I think I'd draw the line there and start to wonder about your sanity. It's the "eating a frog" syndrome.

Let me explain. Have you ever talked to someone in a rational and calm way, and then that person goes off the deep end, saying something so wild that you think you misunderstood the entire conversation? Have you ever been absolutely shocked by the actions of some of your friends, or maybe even of your own? If you've had this experience, you'll probably understand why I liken it to what I call the "eating a frog" syndrome. It's as if everything was fine, and then, in the very middle of "fine," a frog hopped across the floor—and the other person scooped up the frog and ate it. It's bizarre. It seems crazy.

When you find out that your preacher is gay after all that time of his preaching against homosexuality, or that your philosophy professor is a member of a Wicca coven, or that your neighbor who loves kittens is a serial killer, or that your very respectable father is married to two women other than your mother . . . I call that "eating a frog."

The doctrine of the incarnation of God in Christ is crazy—like eating the frog—but in a far different way. It's a surprise, it's astounding, it creates all kinds of questions, and it keeps us awake at night.

The doctrine of the incarnation of God in Christ is the "eating a frog," as it were, aspect of the Christian worldview. I didn't see that for years.

The book of John says, "In the beginning was the Word . . . and the Word was God. . . . And the Word became flesh and dwelt among us" (1:1–14). The writer of Hebrews said, "Long ago, at many times and in many ways, God spoke to our fathers by the prophets, but in these last days he has spoken to us by his Son, whom he appointed the heir of all things, through whom also he created the world. He is the radiance of the glory of God and the exact imprint of his nature, and he upholds the universe by the word of his power" (1:1–3).

The apostle John, who was there when the Gospels' story unfolded, was confident of the truth of Christ's eternal nature and identity as God because of his personal experience with Jesus: "That which was from the beginning, which we have heard, which we have seen with our eyes, which we looked upon and have touched with our hands, concerning the word of life—the life was made manifest, and we have seen it, and testify to it and proclaim to you the eternal life, which was with the Father and was made manifest to us—that which we have seen and heard we proclaim also to you, so that you too may have fellowship with us" (1 John 1:1–3).

The God who is omnipresent (all-present), omnipotent (all-powerful), and omniscient (all-knowing); the God who is the creator, sustainer, and ruler of all that is, became a baby. It's true, but it's weird.

I have just articulated to you the central doctrine of the Christian faith. For much of my teaching and preaching career, I've stopped there.

I didn't go far enough.

Jesus not only is God; he also was a man.

JESUS AS MAN

Let me tell you something quite radical: Jesus wasn't playing games. He didn't say, "Yeah, I'm a man (wink, wink)," knowing that he really was just God in a man suit.

He really was a man.

Most Christians don't have any problem with the God part. It's the man part that drives us nuts. We want Jesus to wear a costume of humanity, but we aren't willing to see his humanity as anything more than a costume. We like the idea of Jesus walking on water, but we have difficulty with his loneliness and his fear. We don't mind the raising of the dead, but we have difficulty with the dirt under the fingernails.

The Bible gives two accounts of the temptation of Jesus. One is in Matthew 4 and the other in Luke 4. A lot of things can be said about Satan's tempting Jesus, but it seems to me that a part of the temptation was Jesus's own question about who he was.

When Jesus talked about the end of all things, he said that he didn't know when it would be. Do you know why he said that? He said it because he really didn't know. When Jesus faced his death, he asked God to prevent it. Do you know why he asked this? He asked because he wanted a way out of that suffering. When Jesus prayed in the garden before his death, the text says that his sweat was like drops of blood. Do you know why? It was because Jesus was really scared.

A major purpose of the incarnation was identification: God identified with us.

I've always talked about the Cross as Christ's self-sacrifice for our sins; I still do. I believe that God showed his love by coming to us in an unfathomable act of condescension. I have always believed that Christians have been declared righteous and justified and that the declaration is legal and settled. I still believe that.

But what I learned by walking with Jesus all this time is his pain. I've learned that he identified with us so totally and so completely that the Scripture says, "We do not have a high priest who is unable to sympathize with our weaknesses, but one who in every respect has been tempted as we are" (Hebrews 4:15). In other words, he didn't play games. When God entered time and space and became human, he really became human.

One of the ancient Christian heresies was called Docetism. It's the view that matter is evil and that God would never condescend to enter an evil human body. The word *Docetism* is derived from the Greek word *dokein*, meaning "to seem." Thus the incarnation was not real. It just seemed real. But that's not what the Bible tells us, and it's not what I believe.

When I go through self-doubt, when I'm afraid, and when I want to avoid the difficult path ahead of me, I tell Jesus, and he says, "I know. Been there, done that." He knows our sufferings. He gets it.

Jesus's Unconditional Love

Once we "get it" in terms of who Jesus is, even that is only a beginning. Frankly, it's just not easy to hang out with Jesus and be a proper Presbyterian. We find out surprising things about the real Jesus that aren't always comfortable. For instance, I noticed that Jesus is a lot more unconditional in his love than I thought he was.

I once thought that Jesus was conditional in his love and acceptance. What was I thinking? I was the one who set conditions.

Jesus said that if we're tired, we can go to him, and he will give us rest—that when our way is hard, his way would be easy (see Matthew 11:28–30). The condition is being tired.

Jesus said that he had come to love sinners (see Matthew 9:13). The condition was being a sinner.

Jesus said that he had come for the sick (see Mark 2:17). The condition was being sick.

Jesus hung out with prostitutes, drunks, and bad people. It quickly becomes clear that if I want to be his friend, I can't be a "proper" Christian.

I serve on two boards, and they both bother me. I've served on the boards of Christian magazines, Christian evangelistic ministries, and Christian sports ministries. I was sort of proud of being on those boards. They defined me as a Christian who is committed to God's work in the world.

Over the last few years, though, I resigned from those boards. I now serve on two boards. One is Harvest USA, started by my friend John Freeman as a ministry to gays and lesbians. Most of the staff and some of the board members at Harvest are homosexuals who are celibate or who have moved into a heterosexual life. When I was asked to serve on that board, I told God that it would hurt my reputation. "God," I said, "people are going to think I'm gay."

JESUS IS A LOT MORE UNCONDITIONAL IN HIS LOVE THAN I THOUGHT HE WAS.

"So?" I think he said in response. "You may not be gay, but you're sinful, dirty, and screwed up. And if they call you gay, be glad, because when people 'utter all kinds of evil against you falsely on my account' (Matthew 5:11), you're to rejoice."

So I winced and signed up.

Then God, in his wisdom and graciousness, gave me another place to serve. I'm also on the board of Victoria's Friends. Victoria

Teague, my friend, is a former strip-club dancer and drug addict. Now, when she goes into strip clubs to minister, she weeps. She remembers the pain of that lifestyle and has incredible compassion for those who still experience that pain.

I told Jesus that I was sort of pleased that he had balanced out the homosexual and heterosexual sin groupings but that I still wasn't altogether happy with where he had sent me. What I had in mind, I told him, was a ministry where "normal" Christians reached out to "normal" people to make them more "normal." "Lord," I said, "what will people say? This could really hurt my reputation and my witness."

"It hurt mine," I think he said. Then he said, "You go, and I'll go with you."

JESUS AND RELIGION

So I went. You see, the only place it really would hurt my reputation was among religious people. I once thought we were called to be religious, but I was wrong. I was the one who took pride in religion. Jesus is far less positive about it than I thought he was.

Some of the harshest words Jesus ever spoke were spoken to and about religious people. He called them hypocrites, narrow-minded, whitewashed tombs, dishonest, and manipulative. He argued with them and told them that they didn't really know or understand the Scriptures. He offended them—he even seemed to go out of his way to offend them. He told stories about them, insulted them, and refused to be more religious to please them.

And he loved them.

In Matthew 5:20 Jesus said something that has always bothered me: "Unless your righteousness exceeds that of the scribes and Pharisees, you will never enter the kingdom of heaven."

Now, before you jump to any conclusions, you need to know that when Jesus said that, the most "righteous" people around were the scribes and Pharisees. You may not want to go to a movie or a football game with them—you may not like them at all—but that doesn't mean that they weren't righteous. These were the folks who came the closest to obeying the law of God—all of it. They were religious professionals who, if they lived today, would be leaders of the church.

If I have to be better than that, I don't stand a chance.

As I mentioned earlier, I'm the host of a syndicated radio talk show. At the time of this writing, a prominent religious leader has advocated the assassination of the president of another country. People who do talk shows *live* for this sort of comment. Everybody else thinks, "How could he?" But a talk show host says, "Cool." We have to find material somewhere.

Just before I started preparing my diatribe about this religious leader's assassination advocacy, someone handed me an article written by another religious leader who declared that this pro-assassination leader was "an embarrassment to the church and a danger to American politics." He went further to say the man was not much different from "Muslim extremists."

Well, I thought, *he may be right, and he probably said it better than I could have said it.* Then I thought, *But how insufferably arrogant and self-righteous he is!*

That's when a question popped into my mind (it may have been God, but I want to be careful here): *And you're not?!*

I thought about the righteousness of the Pharisees and scribes and about how Jesus said that I had to be more righteous than they were. Then I saw what Jesus was saying. He defined righteousness differently than religious people usually define it.

I might be one of the most religious people around, but don't confuse that with righteousness. I once thought that Jesus would be pleased with me because . . . well . . . because he was religious too. Now I'm not so sure. It kind of scares me when I consider the number of times I've used religion as a substitute for God, a method to tell others how good I am, or a badge of honor among the less religious.

Now all of that religiosity isn't looking so good.

A friend of mine says that anybody who makes his or her living at religion is probably going to lose one or the other. I don't totally agree with that, but it's close enough to the truth to cause me to wince. One must be careful about religion, because it can make you feel that you're close to God—that you're pure and that you're serving him—when, in fact, you aren't.

JESUS AND PARTISANSHIP

I once thought that Jesus took sides. But I was wrong. I was the one taking sides. I'm always taking sides. But when I hang out with Jesus, I find that he is far less partisan than I thought he was.

A friend of mine told me many years ago, "Steve, I don't know where you'll be in twenty years, but wherever you are, you'll be waving a flag for something!"

I don't care so much what you believe, but I hope you believe something strongly enough to fight and die for it. If you're a Democrat, don't shilly-shally about your political beliefs. If you're a Republican, be a Republican. If you're a Christian, tell everybody you know and dare them to challenge you. If you're an atheist, be a real one. There's nothing worse than a "weenie" atheist except, maybe, a weenie Christian.

Then I find out that Jesus doesn't choose sides that way. For instance, his criticism of the Pharisees was so harsh that one cannot read it without wincing (see Matthew 23). And yet, on more than one occasion, he went to dinner parties with Pharisees. What's with that?

Jesus reached out to the oppressed and was on the side of the poor while, at the same time, being friends with the oppressors and the ones who helped keep the poor, poor.

He was clear about sexual morality, and in the Sermon on the Mount he went further than the Law did in his comments, saying lust was no better than actual adultery. His teaching on divorce is cut-and-dried—and goes beyond what Moses taught. So what in the world was Jesus doing spending time with adulterers and divorced people?

He lived in the middle of an occupied country, and yet he was often seen reaching out to and loving the occupiers.

It just doesn't make sense.

I'm quite political. On occasion I've been called opinionated. (Well, maybe more than occasionally.) I have

ONE MUST BE CAREFUL ABOUT RELIGION, BECAUSE IT CAN MAKE YOU FEEL THAT YOU'RE CLOSE TO GOD—WHEN, IN FACT, YOU AREN'T.

strong theological, social, and moral convictions and have no hesitation about sharing those views with anyone who will listen. I draw a circle, and I put Republicans, Christians, Presbyterians, and good citizens in the circle and everybody else outside it.

So sometimes I want to say to Jesus, "Just take a side!"

But he doesn't have a side.

I recently spoke at a conference for Christian counselors, who have been criticized by other Christians for being too wishy-washy. At a dinner for the leaders of the conference, I brought up the criticism to see how they would respond. The president said, "While there are many who draw lines, we believe we've been called to build bridges."

Maybe there's something to both methods, and the key is knowing when to draw lines and when to build bridges.

Jesus drew lines, and they were clear, absolute, and hard. I knew that. But he also crossed every one of those lines and loved people on the other side.

The more I walk with him, the more I'm learning to see people through his eyes. That means I'm called to reach out to people who aren't the kind of people I want to know, people who are on the other side of the line. In other words, I like Republicans and Presbyterians; but the more I walk with Jesus, the more I understand that he probably wouldn't spend as much time with them as I do.

JESUS'S OPEN INVITATION

I once thought that Jesus's invitation was pretty exclusive. But I was the one who was into exclusivity. His invitation is far more open than I thought it was.

One wonderful image in the Bible is the marriage supper of the Lamb. Jesus referred to it at the last meal he shared with his disciples before his crucifixion. Revelation 19:6–9 gives a wonderful description of that marriage supper:

Then I heard what seemed to be the voice of a great multitude, like the roar of many waters and like the sound of mighty peals of thunder, crying out,

> "Hallelujah!
> For the Lord our God
>   the Almighty reigns.
> Let us rejoice and exult
>   and give him the glory,
> for the marriage of the Lamb has come,
>   and his Bride has made herself ready;
> it was granted her to clothe herself
>   with fine linen, bright and pure"—

for the fine linen is the righteous deeds of the saints.

And the angel said to me, "Write this: Blessed are those who are invited to the marriage supper of the Lamb."

I used to think that the marriage supper of the Lamb would be like a covered-dish supper at the local Protestant church: great food, good people, and the security of knowing that our fellowship is with those who belong to God.

C. M. Ward, the great Assemblies of God preacher and voice of the old *Revival Time* radio program, was one of my favorite preachers long before I started believing anything he said. Even as a teenager I was fascinated with his ability to effortlessly put together a long list of adjectives relating to God and the things of God. As I remember it, Ward often closed his broadcast by talking about the "long, long altar, where there is room enough for you."

I think the marriage supper of the Lamb will be like that. It will have a long, long table, and there's room enough for you.

That table will include those who were murderers, thieves, liars, adulterers, homosexuals, politicians, lawyers, tax collectors, prostitutes, drug addicts, and strippers.

I know what you're thinking: *Wait, wait. You don't mean to tell me that the marriage supper of the Lamb will include people like that?!*

Yes, the marriage supper of the Lamb will include people "like that"—people whose lives were once full of sin but who have been forgiven and redeemed. After all, it's going to include, I'm told, people like me.

It will include arrogant Christians whose self-righteousness will be hard to maintain in that kind of company. Some there might once have found it difficult to reconcile their theological views with the people they'll be sitting alongside. Some at that table may be the religious who would normally want to close their eyes and pretend that "those" folks aren't there. We'll undoubtedly find at that table preachers, elders, deacons, and leaders of the church who believed that the church was an institution. Sprinkled in will be some who have Sunday-school attendance pins that reach down to the floor.

The marriage supper of the Lamb will be for sinners like all of us.

It's a long, long table.

And there's room enough for you!

I used to think there wasn't.

I was wrong.

MANY ARE DECEIVED IN THE END,
WHO AT FIRST SEEMED TO BE LED BY THE HOLY SPIRIT.

THOMAS À KEMPIS

The Holy Spirit Is Working in a Lot More Places Than I Thought He Was

O Lord, you have searched me and known me! You know when I sit down and when I rise up; you discern my thoughts from afar. You search out my path and my lying down and are acquainted with all my ways. . . . Where shall I go from your Spirit?

PSALM 139:1–7

The Holy Spirit is a lot busier than I thought he was. Right now, he might be in places you never expected, doing things you never anticipated, and acting in rather shocking ways.

I used to have a very limited view of the Holy Spirit. What was I thinking?

I once wrote a book about the Holy Spirit titled *Follow the Wind*.[1] In it I attempted to convey what the Bible says about the Holy Spirit, and I stand by what I wrote.

If you read it, you'll learn a lot about the Holy Spirit, the history of the doctrine of the Holy Spirit in the church, and the work of the Holy Spirit in the believer and in the world. The book deals with some of the controversies about the Holy Spirit in church history and with some of the modern controversies about the gift of tongues, the "baptism" of the Holy Spirit, and the work of the Holy Spirit in the sanctification of the Christian.

If you want to know the truth about the Holy Spirit, I highly recommend that book. After all, I'm not above trying to sell books to earn a little extra money. (Actually, the ministry for which I work and which gets the profits from all my books, Key Life, needs the money.) So buy it—I think you'll like it.

However, if you want to know everything I've discovered about the Holy Spirit, you won't find it in that book.

One of the interesting things about the Holy Spirit is his job description. He never points to himself; instead, he always points to the first person (God the Father) and the second person (God the Son) of the Trinity. In John 15:26 Jesus said this about the Holy Spirit: "When the Helper comes, whom I will send to you from the Father, the Spirit of truth, who proceeds from the Father, he will bear witness about me."

In John 16:14–15 Jesus said, "He will glorify me, for he will take what is mine and declare it to you. All that the Father has is mine; therefore I said that he will take what is mine and declare it to you."

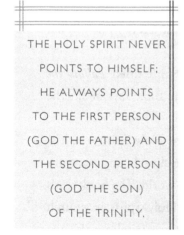

THE HOLY SPIRIT NEVER POINTS TO HIMSELF; HE ALWAYS POINTS TO THE FIRST PERSON (GOD THE FATHER) AND THE SECOND PERSON (GOD THE SON) OF THE TRINITY.

So it's risky business to start talking about the Holy Spirit. We can miss him in a lot of places.

The late H. R. Rookmaaker, a professor at Free University of Amsterdam, would, I'm told, show two paintings to his classes. One of the paintings would be clearly religious and might portray Jesus on the cross. The other would not be religious, in the sense that it portrayed no religious subject. Then he would ask his students which of the paintings was Christian.

The students would, of course, point to the overtly religious painting. That's when Dr. Rookmaaker would explain that the true Christian painting was not necessarily the one with the cross but rather whichever one reflected integrity, power, and beauty and that glorified God, from whom those things flow.[2]

Of course the Holy Spirit has a special place in the lives of believers. He guides, comforts, reveals truth, teaches, convicts, applies God's Word, gives spiritual gifts, and manifests the fruit of the Spirit (love, joy, peace, patience, kindness, goodness, faithfulness, gentleness, and self-control). The Holy Spirit interprets believers' prayers before the throne of God; lifts up, honors, and glorifies the Father and the Son; guides the church; and does a whole lot more.

You knew that.

The fact is, if you've been a Christian for very long, you've been taught about the Holy Spirit. Perhaps you even know more about the Holy Spirit than most Christians do. But, as Paul Harvey says, "You know the story . . . now let me tell you the rest of the story."

The Holy Spirit's work is not limited to Christians and the church.

"Secular" and "sacred" are categories that enable us to separate "us" from "them" or to divide our lives into "God stuff" and "not God stuff." However, those categories are not biblical categories. The Scriptures never put God in a box of the "sacred." Nothing is beyond his domain. He isn't just the ruler of a place; he's the ruler of *all* places. He isn't just the sustainer of religious stuff; he's the sustainer of *all* stuff. He isn't just the master of his own people; he's the master of *everyone*. Consider:

- "To the LORD your God belong heaven and the heaven of heavens, the earth with all that is in it." (Deuteronomy 10:14)

- "Blessed be the name of God forever and ever, to whom belong wisdom and might. He changes times and seasons; he removes kings and sets up kings; he gives wisdom to the wise and knowledge to those who have understanding." (Daniel 2:20–21)

- "O LORD God of hosts, who is mighty as you are, O LORD, with your faithfulness all around you? You rule the raging of the sea; when its waves rise, you still them. . . . The heavens are yours; the earth also is yours; the world and all that is in it, you have founded them. The north and the south, you have created them." (Psalm 89:8–12)

The Bible is a covenant book for God's covenant people. The Holy Spirit is, in a very particular and important way, the gift God gives to his people. Jesus said, "I will ask the Father, and he will give you another Helper, to be with you forever, even the Spirit of truth, whom the world cannot receive, because it neither sees him nor knows him. You know him, for he dwells with you and will be in you" (John 14:16–17).

But while the Bible is a covenant book for God's covenant people, it would be a disastrous mistake to think of God as only the God of the church or to think of God's chief concern as religion. If God is sovereign over all his creation, it stands to reason that he is acting everywhere he rules. And that, of course, is everywhere.

In the Old Testament, the word for God's Spirit is *Ruah*, and it means both breath and wind. The Holy Spirit, the Bible teaches, is God's power in action, or God's energy let loose. If that's true—and the Bible clearly states that it is—then the Holy Spirit is operating in a whole lot of places we might not expect.

THE ACTIVITY OF THE HOLY SPIRIT

Let me share with you five areas in which the Bible teaches that the Holy Spirit is active. This may seem rather pedantic and dull, but if you'll stay with me, we'll see some incredible implications of the Holy Spirit's involvement in those areas.

1. *The Holy Spirit Is Active in Creation*

The first place we encounter the Holy Spirit in the Bible is in the opening verses of the first chapter of Genesis, the first book of the Bible. Those verses say that God created everything, and they give us a glimpse of what it was like before God created: "The earth was without form and void, and darkness was over the face of the deep. And the Spirit of God was hovering over the face of the waters" (Genesis 1:2).

In creating the first human being in Genesis 2, the Spirit was active: "The LORD God formed the man of dust from the ground and breathed into his nostrils the breath [the word for *Spirit*] of life, and the man became a living creature" (Genesis 2:7). The psalmist said, "By the word of the LORD the heavens were made, and by the breath [there it is again] of his mouth all their host" (Psalm 33:6). The psalmist also stated, "When you send forth your Spirit, they are created, and you renew the face of the ground" (Psalm 104:30).

2. *The Holy Spirit Teaches and Affirms Truth*

Jesus called the Holy Spirit the "Spirit of truth" (John 14:17). Then he expanded on that by saying, "The Helper, the Holy Spirit, whom the Father will send in my name, he will teach you all things and bring to your remembrance all that I have said to you" (John 14:26).

Jesus also said about the Holy Spirit, "When the Spirit of truth comes, he will guide you into all the truth" (John 16:13).

The apostle Paul said that the Holy Spirit lives within believers and that he is a sort of truth detector. Paul wrote, "These things God has revealed to us through the Spirit. For the Spirit searches everything, even the depths of God. For who knows a person's thoughts except the spirit of that person, which is in him? So also no one comprehends the thoughts of God except the Spirit of God. Now we have received not the spirit of the world, but the Spirit who is from God, that we might understand the things freely given us by God" (1 Corinthians 2:10–12).

3. *The Holy Spirit Creates Righteousness*

In Isaiah 61 the year of the Lord's favor was proclaimed. This, by the way, is the passage Jesus read at the synagogue in Nazareth (Luke 4:16–22), adding, "Today this Scripture has been fulfilled in your hearing" (Luke 4:21). In Luke, quoting the Isaiah passage, Jesus said, "The Spirit of the Lord is upon me" (Luke 4:18). This simple yet provocative statement is followed by a list of what is proclaimed and accomplished by the Spirit of the Lord's anointing: "He has anointed me to proclaim good news to the poor. He has sent me to proclaim liberty to the captives and recovering of sight to the blind, to set at liberty those who are oppressed, to proclaim the year of the Lord's favor" (Luke 4:18–19). But further along in the Isaiah passage is this additional function of the Holy Spirit's anointing: "That they may be called oaks of righteousness, the planting of the LORD, that he may be glorified" (Isaiah 61:3).

The first chapter of Ezra opens with these words: "In the first year of Cyrus king of Persia, that the word of the LORD by the mouth of Jeremiah might be fulfilled, the LORD stirred up the spirit of Cyrus king of Persia" (Ezra 1:1). In Isaiah 45:1, that same Cyrus is called God's "anointed" (anointed, I presume, by God's Spirit) who will fulfill God's purpose. Cyrus was the king of Persia and not a part of the covenant community of God, yet the Holy Spirit anointed Cyrus and used him to accomplish God's righteous plan.

Then, in Galatians, Paul talks about righteousness—"love, joy, peace, patience, kindness, goodness, faithfulness, gentleness, self-control"—as "fruit of the Spirit" (Galatians 5:22–23). While the fruit of the Spirit primarily is produced in the Christian in whom the Spirit dwells, one can safely say that wherever the Holy Spirit works in the world, we can see the same fruit.

4. *The Holy Spirit Originates and Inspires Beauty so That God May Be Glorified*

When God gave Moses instructions for creating the art and beauty of the Tent of Meeting (the tabernacle), he was not just concerned with function and form but also with beauty. The Holy Spirit would inspire God's anointed craftsmen to make beautiful the place where God would meet with his people. In Exodus 31:1–5 God told Moses, "See, I have called by name Bezalel the son of Uri, son of Hur, of the tribe of Judah, and I have filled him with the Spirit of God, with ability and intelligence, with knowledge and all craftsmanship, to devise artistic designs, to work in gold, silver, and bronze, in cutting stones for setting, and in carving wood, to work in every craft."

In the book of the prophet Haggai, God called to mind the glory of the temple that had been destroyed. God promised to restore the temple to its former beauty and glory. Through Haggai, he said, "Who is left among you who saw this house in its former glory? How do you see it now? Is it not as nothing in your eyes? Yet now be strong. . . . Be strong, all you people of the land, declares the LORD. Work, for I am with you, declares the LORD of hosts, according to the covenant that I made with you when you came out of Egypt. My Spirit remains in your midst. Fear not" (Haggai 2:3–5).

5. *The Holy Spirit Works in People*

Finally, the Holy Spirit works in people to give them an awareness of truth and to draw them to God.

In Jesus's rather long teaching about the Holy Spirit in John 16, he said, among other things, "When he comes, he will convict the world concerning sin and righteousness and judgment: concerning sin, because they do not believe in me; concerning righteousness, because I go to the Father, and you will see me no longer; concerning judgment, because the ruler of this world is judged" (John 16:8–11).

THE HOLY SPIRIT AND RELIGION

Got it? Creation, truth, goodness, beauty, and reality. If you've got that, we can "boldly go where no one has gone before"—or, at least, where very few Christians will go.

Henry P. Van Dusen, once president of Union Seminary in New York, wrote extensively about the Holy Spirit. He identified the modern-day Pentecostal movement (a movement that takes seriously the supernatural work of the Holy Spirit) as a "new reformation." He called it a kind of third force, standing alongside Roman Catholicism and historic Protestantism in its significance.

While I have some serious differences with Dr. Van Dusen about some of the things he said and wrote, his comment on the Holy Spirit's work in the world is so profound that I must tell you what he said. He wrote, "[Those of us who] cleave to the Scriptural conviction that God has not left Himself without witness, at any time or among any people, [will] find abundant confirmation of that belief in the awareness of His Spirit—however dim and however crude—in the consciousness of humanity virtually everywhere and always."[3]

> WE ARE FAR TOO RELIGIOUS. THE PROBLEM IS THAT THE HOLY SPIRIT ISN'T.

Now, let me get to my main point. One of the great dangers for Christians and for the world is that we are far, far too religious. We go to religious movies, we read religious books, we associate with religious people, we eat religious cookies, and we wear religious underwear that is far too tight. Our problem is that we spend too much time in church and far too little time in "the world." Jesus said that we are like leaven, and that's true. As someone has said, though, we have become a "lump of leaven," and lumps of leaven are no good to anybody.

Don't get me wrong. I'm religious too. The problem is that the Holy Spirit isn't.

We linger far longer than we should at church, thinking that's where God would have us stay. But it isn't. We should be there, but not for long. The church should be the "gasoline station," not the place where we park the car. When Jesus said that we are to "go into all the world" (Mark 16:15), he didn't say that we should stay at the "gas station" holding hands and thanking the service manager for filling our tanks. He was saying that he planned to "leave the building"—and that we should go with him.

You're probably saying, "But of course. That's what Christians do. We share the gospel. We go on the mission field and reach out to the world with compassion and love." Yes, that's true, and that's a part of it. But being a Christian is far more than that, and what we're going to talk about shortly may shock you.

It has shocked me, and I like to spread the shock around.

RUNNING FROM THE WORLD

Let me deal with an issue that Christians have long used to run from the world. Paul wrote to the church at Corinth, "Do not be unequally yoked with unbelievers. For what partnership has righteousness with lawlessness? Or what fellowship has light with darkness? What accord has Christ with Belial? Or what portion does a believer share with an unbeliever? What agreement has the temple of God with idols?" (2 Corinthians 6:14–16).

It's important that we understand what Paul meant. Fortunately, we don't even have to ask; he told us. In fact, in 1 Corinthians 5:9–11 Paul referred to what he had written previously. (The time line of 1 and 2 Corinthians is a bit skewed in our present manuscripts. Many scholars think that some of 2 Corinthians actually came before 1 Corinthians.) Paul said this: "I wrote to you in my letter not to associate with sexually immoral people—not at all meaning the sexually immoral of this world, or the greedy and swindlers, or idolaters, since then you would need to go out of the world. But now I am writing to you not to associate with anyone who bears the name of brother if he is guilty of sexual immorality or greed, or is an idolater, reviler, drunkard, or swindler—not even to eat with such a one." Then Paul goes on to say that his admonition had to do with Christians who betray the name of Christ—not with the world, where betrayal is rather difficult given the fact that these people don't even know Christ.

Various studies have shown that believers are as involved in and as affected by popular culture as anyone else. Christians, in about the same numbers as non-Christians, attend concerts, go to museums, and watch the same television programs as everybody else. I'm involved in and affirm the ministry of Christian media; but if numbers are any indication, Christian media have far less impact on professing Christians than mainstream media do. In fact, if just the Christians in America listened to and watched Christian media, the ratings would be phenomenal. They aren't.

In other words, Christians are just about like everyone else in terms of their involvement in and their support of "worldly" culture.

That's bad!

No, that's good. And I'm going to tell you why.

Bach, Bubba, and the Blues Brothers

Reggie Kidd, my friend and colleague at Reformed Theological Seminary, where I teach, wrote a profound and wonderful book about worship, *With One Voice: Discovering Christ's Song in Our*

Worship.[4] This book is, I believe, one of the most important popular books on worship ever written.

Reggie and I team-teach a Theology of Ministry course, and in his lectures Reggie often refers to various forms of music used in worship. In that course (and in his book), he describes those forms of worship as "Bach, Bubba, and the Blues Brothers."

He is, of course, teaching the many voices of worship.

The interesting thing about Reggie's lectures is that he often uses secular music, imagery, and art to illustrate what he's teaching. I asked Reggie (who has a PhD from Duke) how he knew what was good and what was bad in terms of culture. He said that if one's worldview is right (i.e., if one has a biblical worldview), then almost anything can be used to reflect and glorify God. He also said that if one's worldview is not stable, then everything else is dangerous.

> IT'S WHAT WE BRING TO WHERE WE GO, TO WHAT WE SEE, AND TO WHAT WE HEAR THAT DETERMINES WHAT IS APPROPRIATE AND RIGHT FOR US AS BELIEVERS.

Recently Reggie went to a U2 concert. He later kidded that it was so wonderful that he wouldn't have to go to church for the next two months.

That brings me to say something I believe to be biblical, surprising, and exciting: It isn't where we go, what we see, and what we hear that determines what is appropriate and right for a believer. It's what we bring to where we go, to what we see, and to what we hear that determines what is appropriate and right for us as believers.

I can hear you saying, "Steve, that can't be right!" Oh, yes, it is. I didn't say it; God did: "To the pure, all things are pure" (Titus 1:15).

In writing about popular culture, William Romanowski, professor of communication arts and sciences at Calvin College, wrote something that's applicable to believers and our relationship with all kinds of cultural and "worldly" expressions:

> Limiting Christian criticism of the popular arts to confessional and moral content has fostered an understanding of popular art in terms of good/bad, right/wrong dichotomy. Consequently, many Christians have a difficult time evaluating popular art beyond the most superficial level. . . . We have not thought deeply enough about the nature of popular art and its role as a cultural communicator, which leaves us with very little to contribute to the discourse about popular art and culture. In varying ways, these approaches prohibit believers from distinguishing redemptive aspects of popular culture, determining appropriate Christian participation, and developing tools for constructive criticism.[5]

Leland Ryken addressed the same issue in his book on the arts. He wrote:

> Involvement in the arts allows Christians to respond to their surrounding culture. Christians are responsible to be a redemptive influence in their culture. That responsibility begins by understanding their culture, including its artistic expressions.[6]

The Russian novelist Fyodor Dostoyevsky wrote that "man has no right to turn back and to ignore what is going on in the world—and there are supreme moral reasons for not allowing him to do so."

THE HOLY SPIRIT AND THE WORLD

I don't know about you, but church is comfortable for me. The people there talk the way I talk, believe what I believe, dislike what I dislike, and affirm all that I hold dear. When I venture into other places, even if it's God's Spirit who leads me there, I'm uncomfortable and afraid. We don't venture much outside the church because we're sure that the world is dirty, angry, wrong, and maybe even a bit too tempting.

When I was growing up, I was not the best student. Well, that may be an understatement. I was a horrible student—rebellious, bored, and distracted. I was trouble looking for a place to happen. It was rare (so rare that it happened only once) for me to have a teacher who was even worse at teaching than I was at learning. In third grade, however, one teacher singled me out as the object of her wrath.

I went to school in an era when the teacher was always right. If I complained to my mother about a teacher, my mother would discipline *me*. If I questioned a teacher, my mother always took the teacher's side. And if I ever came home with a note from a teacher about my bad conduct in class, that note might as well have been from Sinai, the "mountain of God." Teachers were without fault and well respected. If I ever had a problem with a teacher—no matter what the circumstances were—it was assumed to be my problem, certainly not the teacher's.

I didn't find out until I was an adult that there had been one major exception. As I mentioned earlier, my third-grade teacher was abusive and angry, and it seemed she directed all her abuse and anger at me. I could do nothing right. I found it impossible to please her. I tried. I really tried to please her . . . but to no avail.

I suppose my mother noticed my black mood (mothers do notice such things). Perhaps she heard me crying. Maybe she just knew my heart and knew when it was broken and afraid. She asked me what was wrong, and at great personal risk to my own well-being, I told her about the teacher. She said, "Son, she's your teacher, and I don't expect to hear anything about her again."

It was settled. I would just have to deal with it.

Then something strange happened. The next week that teacher changed. It was like she'd taken a "nice" pill or something. Whereas before I had been the brunt of her anger, jokes, and abuse, I now seemed to be her favorite person in the world—and I hadn't even given her an apple. She praised my work in front of the class, told me how nice I looked, and even, on occasion, hugged me.

Frankly, that made me a bit uncomfortable. Even at that young age, I figured my teacher must be drunk.

She wasn't.

She had, however, received a visit from my mother. You don't know my mother, but if you did, you would know that this was not a woman you'd want to cross. The only person I knew who could be meaner and more dangerous than my teacher was my mother. If my mother had a "come to Jesus" meeting with you, all you wanted to do was repent and run. When my mother was angry, she could spit on the grass and it would wither. (My mother was the earthiest Christian I've ever known. She loved

Jesus, and she loved my brother and me without reservation or exception. The fact that it didn't always feel like love was a tribute to the kind of love with which she loved us. I know of no person, with the possible exception of my wife, who has had a greater and more positive influence on my life and my walk with God than my mother.)

Anyway, I was never privy to the conversation that took place between my mother and that teacher. Knowing my mother, I do know that whatever she said wasn't subtle. My mother was not a subtle woman. I suspect it was something like, "Do you like being a teacher? If you do, you will stop abusing my son. If you don't, I'll make sure you never teach again." Possibly my mother said, "You mess with my son again and I'll break your face!" All I knew was that the meanest teacher I'd ever had became the nicest.

Why am I telling you this? Because that's what the Holy Spirit has done in the world. The Holy Spirit has sent you into the world, and when you go, you'll find that he has gone before you. If you're willing to risk, you'll be surprised at how much creativity, truth, goodness, and beauty is out there. Not only that, but you'll also find that people—people out there—have a great yearning for God.

Is "out there" a dangerous place? Are you crazy? Of course it is. Christians get killed "out there." Great darkness, greed, and lust can be found "out there." You'll find selfishness and hatred of God and of anything or anyone associated with God . . . like us, for instance. Perversion is out there, and egos so big that there's no room for truth, goodness, or beauty.

But in the midst of that mud, there are diamonds.

NOW FOR THE SHOCK

Now for the shocking part: If you're a Christian, Jesus did not remove you from the world. Nor, believe it or not, does he keep you from enjoying it.

Contrary to a lot of Christian drivel, just because you like something doesn't mean it's sin. And if you don't like something, that doesn't necessarily mean it's good for you. In fact, it could be that the opposite is true. The Holy Spirit is doing great things in the world, yet we are in great danger of missing it—and him. We're also in danger of walking away from the world's culture at the very point at which, if we speak with authenticity and humility, our message just might be heard.

> EVERYWHERE YOU GO, YOU'LL FIND THE HOLY SPIRIT CREATING BEAUTY, REVEALING TRUTH, MANIFESTING GOODNESS, AND STIRRING A HUNGER FOR THE REALITY OF GOD.

Don Richardson, in his book *Eternity in Their Hearts*, makes the point that wherever missionaries go they find that God has been there first, going before them.[7] It's time we made the same discovery about wherever we may go in the world.

The Holy Spirit works in churches. But never forget that he's also working in bars and theaters, in ballparks and stadiums, in museums and concert halls, in politics and government, in novels and journals. In short, our Lord the Holy Spirit has gone wherever believers can go. Everywhere you go, you'll find the Holy Spirit creating beauty, revealing truth, manifesting goodness, and stirring a hunger for the reality of God.

Christians are human beings who rejoice in God's creation and who, with other human beings, enjoy the fruits of culture. We *are* human beings, but we are also more than that. We're human beings in whom the Holy Spirit (who is working in the world) resides. The Holy Spirit, by his very presence in our lives, gives us (even if we don't know it) a "baloney detector." While there is much evil in our culture, there's much good too. We've been given the gift of knowing the difference.

Our gift to the world is to show up and engage. Too often we've run *from* the world when we ought to run *toward* it. Our gift to the world is not one of anger, judgment, or condemnation. Our gift to the world is to find where the Holy Spirit is creating beauty, speaking truth, and manifesting goodness—and when we find it, to identify it, enjoy it, affirm it, and get involved in it.

Paul said, "Finally, brothers, whatever is true, whatever is honorable, whatever is just, whatever is pure, whatever is lovely, whatever is commendable, if there is any excellence, if there is anything worthy of praise, think about these things" (Philippians 4:8).

Good heavens! I always thought he was talking about religion.

I was wrong.

I'm going to a movie.

So there.

FOUL SHAME AND SCORN BE ON YE ALL
WHO TURN THE GOOD TO EVIL,
AND STEAL THE BIBLE FROM THE LORD
AND GIVE IT TO THE DEVIL.

John Greenleaf Whittier

The Bible Reveals a Lot More Than I Thought It Did

*In that day the deaf shall hear the words of a book, and out of their
gloom and darkness the eyes of the blind shall see.
The meek shall obtain fresh joy in the LORD, and the poor among
mankind shall exult in the Holy One of Israel.*

ISAIAH 29:18–19

IN HIS BOOK *Journey into Light*, the late Émile Cailliet wrote about
his first encounter with the Bible. His philosophical naturalism
had prevented him from considering God or theology. However,
Cailliet knew there had to be something more than what he had
experienced. He had tried to compose a book that expressed who
he was by writing down quotes he had read from a variety of
sources that had resonated with him. As he read through the book
he had compiled, he recognized the futility of his efforts and was
quite depressed.

Earlier his wife had visited a French Huguenot chapel, and
the pastor had given her a Bible. When she saw her husband so
despondent, she hesitantly (knowing his views on religion) offered
the Bible. Cailliet had never seen a Bible before, but he wrote:

> I literally grabbed the book and rushed to my study with it. I
> opened it and chanced upon the beatitudes! I read, and read,
> and read—now aloud with an indescribable warmth surging

within. . . . I could not find words to express my awe and wonder. And suddenly the realization dawned upon me: This was the book that would understand me—I needed it so much, yet, unaware, I had attempted to write my own—in vain. I continued to read deeply into the night, mostly from the Gospels. And lo and behold, as I looked through them, the One of whom they spoke, the One who spoke and acted in them, became alive to me. . . . While it seemed absurd to speak of a book understanding a man, this could be said of the Bible because its pages were animated by the presence of the living God and the power of his mighty acts. To this God I prayed that night, and the God who answered was the same God of whom it was spoken in the Book.[1]

Cailliet then described how, as he read the Gospels, the One about whom they spoke became real to him. In other words, he discovered the Bible and then became a Christian by reading the Bible. It often happens that way.

That's not what happened to me.

It might surprise you to know that I became a Christian long before I believed in or took the Bible very seriously. I thought I was an intellectual, and I thought intellectuals were immune to the silly religiosity of the Bible. I didn't believe in things like seas that parted, virgin births, or resurrections.

French mathematician and religious philosopher Blaise Pascal said he would never have found God if God had not already found him. I guess that was true for me, even if I didn't know it. I had a spiritual hunger, and that hunger presupposed the existence of food to satisfy it. I had a sense of guilt, and that guilt presupposed the existence of someone who could forgive me. I wanted meaning in my life, and that desire presupposed that something beyond me was the source of meaning. Even intellectuals eventually will die, and most are not altogether happy about the prospect. I wanted to have some kind of hope that my life would not come to an abrupt end in a graveyard.

Then Jesus came.

I didn't know much about Jesus except what I had learned in Sunday school as a child, but I suppose that was enough. When I really got to know Jesus, the spiritual hunger I had felt was somewhat bearable; I felt forgiven; I found a modicum of meaning. And while I didn't want to ask too many questions about it, I thought there might be something on the other side of the grave.

Jesus did that for me, but the Bible was something else altogether. The theological education I received at a very liberal graduate school at a major university didn't help me appreciate the Bible much. In fact, my professors almost took away the minimal relationship I had with Jesus along with any possibility of my having a Cailliet-like experience with Scripture.

It's a long story, and I won't bore you with the details, but because of some wonderful people who really were intellectuals— people who had read all the books I'd read, knew all the words I knew, *and* believed in the Bible—I came to the position that I now hold and have held for most of my adult life: the Bible is the absolute Word of God. I believe and teach the verbal plenary inspiration of Scripture (*verbal* referring to the words and *plenary* meaning all of it—thus, every word of the Bible is true), and I believe the Bible to be revealed propositional truth and to be accurate in everything it affirms.

Because the journey from where I was (a liberal this side of crazy) to where I ended up (believing in the full authority of the Bible) was such a rigorous and difficult one, when I got there I spent a considerable portion of my time simply holding, as it were, the land I had acquired.

Today I'm quite good at defending the eternal verity of the Bible and biblical truth. If you should visit my study, you would note that a large section of my library is devoted to the defense of the inspiration and authority of the canon of Scripture.

But I haven't been to that section of my library much lately. And I want to tell you why.

You may be thinking that it's because I've changed my views. Not even close. In fact, my views on biblical authority are, if anything, stronger and more firmly settled in my mind and heart than ever. Those views are the anchor of how I define myself. One doesn't give up what one has worked so hard to attain.

> WE CAN BE SO ENAMORED WITH THE BIBLE'S TRUTH THAT WE FORGET THAT THE TRUTH IS TO BE LIVED AND USED, NOT JUST ACQUIRED AND MEMORIZED.

In attaining the doctrinal position I now hold, my problem was that I had lost something extremely important. The liberals tried to take away the Bible's import with the unbelief they fostered. They needn't have bothered. My high view of Scripture and my unrelenting defense of its truth had done the same thing to me that the liberals had done so many years before: it robbed me of the power, the reality, and the joy of the Bible. You see, I had made the Bible too religious. I had put a candle on each side of it and placed it on an altar in my heart and dared anybody to mess with it.

A friend of mine says that much of the evangelism and witnessing done by Christians is a pyramid scheme. The purpose is to acquire the product (i.e., salvation), sell it to others, and then train those others to sell it . . . so those others will, in turn, acquire it and train others to sell it. The problem, my friend says, is that nobody ever uses the product. We just sell it.

That's a good point.

It can be true with the Bible too. We can spend so much time defending and "selling" the Bible to others that we don't use the product very much. And we can spend so much time articulating and defending our doctrinal position from the Bible that we forget why it was even important in the first place. Just as it's easy to eat so many doughnuts that we forget how good they taste, we can be so enamored with the Bible's truth that we forget that the truth is to be lived and used, not just acquired and memorized.

I want to share with you some things about the Bible that are more important than what I just told you . . . and maybe some things that will be more important than what you already knew.

Let's start with the bad news, and then it will get better.

THE BIBLE ISN'T A MAGIC PILL

The Bible is not a magic book to put under our pillow at night to make all our bad dreams go away. The Bible was never meant to be worshiped or to be used as a magic cure-all to fix everything that's wrong.

I'm sure you've heard advice like this: Are you depressed? Read the Bible. Are you falling into temptation? Memorize Scripture. Are you scared? Read the Bible through in a year. Do you struggle with obedience? You're simply not studying the Word enough. Do you have doubts? Just keep reading until your doubts go away. Are you trying to be a better mother, father, husband, or wife but failing miserably? The solution is the Bible, and your problem is that you've gone everywhere else but there for help.

In other words, fill your mind with the Bible (i.e., take the magic pill), and there won't be room for any of the bad stuff.

What? That's crazy. First, it's not true. Second, it grossly underestimates the human capacity for multitasking.

I know more of the Bible and have memorized more of it than, I think it's fair to say, the majority of people have. That's not pride (well, maybe a little); it's simply a statement of fact. It's part of what I do for a living. I've been a Bible teacher for most of my adult life. I can hardly think a thought without thinking of a biblical text. If the Bible were the magic book we've been taught it is, I would be far more spiritual and obedient and far less frightened and angry than the majority of people, but I'm not. I may even be worse.

People who believe the way I do about the Bible often use this slogan: "God said it, I believe it, and that settles it for me." It sounds nice, but that doesn't settle it for me anymore. I've been asking an important question: so what? Just believing it because God said it used to settle it for me, but as of late it doesn't even come close. There are, however, some things (even if they don't settle it) that make it better.

THE BIBLE ISN'T JUST ABOUT RELIGION

I feel better, for instance, when I remember that the Bible is actually far less religious than I thought it was.

It might surprise you to learn that the Bible's original language had to be "cleaned up" in our modern translations because . . . well . . . because it would offend the sensitive tastes of "nice Christians." We take a book of the Bible about sex and make it a book about the church. We sanitize the imagery in the Bible and "fix" the "inappropriate" parts. (I would go into detail here, but I simply cannot . . . because of my very point!) We often simply ignore the numerous warts of Bible characters. We take the common Greek of the New Testament (Koinê), formalize it, bring it into the church, and make it hallowed as if it had been dropped out of the sky in a golden wrapper.

I have a minister friend whose young pastoral associate usually read the designated scriptures during the church worship services. The problem was, the associate hardly ever read the passage ahead of time, in preparation. My friend decided to break him of that habit, so one week he assigned a reading that included some rather earthy verses not usually read in public worship services. (Oh yes, there are a number of those.)

The young associate stood before the congregation and started reading. When he realized what he was reading, he started blushing, stumbling over the words, and pausing in places where a pause wasn't necessary. He got through it, but he never read a text "cold" again.

If you haven't blushed, been shocked and embarrassed, and said to yourself, *I don't believe I would have said that*, then you've probably read more nursery rhymes than Bible texts.

At certain times in the church's history, some believed the Bible was so sacred that it should not even be read by "common" people. The thought was that if people read the Bible without the proper interpretation, it would be dangerous. How ironic, when you consider that for the most part, the Bible was written by common people—common people under the inspiration of God's Spirit.

Eventually some godly servants of Christ (some of whom lost their lives for their trouble) worked to translate the Bible into the language of common people so everyone could read it for himself or herself. Martin Luther's translation of the Scriptures into German changed the religious and cultural landscape. Luther spent a considerable portion of time in nearby towns and markets listening to how people spoke because he wanted to make sure they would be able to understand his translation. He said that when he finished his translation, the gospel would be understood by a farm boy behind a plow as well as by the scholars and the priests at a university.

My point is this: we must avoid the pitfalls and danger of taking the Bible back to where it was before these Reformers succeeded in translating the Bible into the common languages. Of course we wouldn't translate it back into Greek, Hebrew, Aramaic, or Latin. The danger is that we'll translate the Bible into the language of "holy," and nobody will want to have anything to do with it if they don't speak "holy."

THE BIBLE IS ABOUT REAL PEOPLE

I also feel better when I remember that the Bible has a far more realistic view of humans and of the world itself than I once believed.

Many people think the Bible is a book written to tell us about the lives and teachings of radically spiritual and super believers who had it all together because of their extreme spirituality. But nothing could be further from the truth. The Bible was written (under the inspiration of the Holy Spirit, of course) by people who were as scared, depressed, sinful, doubting, flawed, and human as we are. Some of them wanted nothing more than to run from their calling. Some even questioned whether God had truly called them to write.

The people of the Bible—those who wrote, those who spoke, and those whose stories unfold on its pages—are not superheroes who will inspire you to be a superhero yourself. They are people like you and me who discovered a merciful, kind, and sovereign God—one who cared enough about their humanity to come as a baby in a dirty stable.

If you ever want to feel better about yourself, read what the Bible has to say about certain members of the family of God. You might find yourself saying, "Well, I may be bad, but I'm not that bad!" (And when you really understand, you'll repent for saying it.) The fact is that sometimes these "Bible heroes" were a bunch of reprobates and scoundrels. If you want to hear from people who have it together and will tell you how you can get it together too, the Bible is not your book. If you want to find out how to be more religious and nicer, good luck trying to force the Bible into that mold. It's not a manual for the religious or the nice.

> THE PEOPLE OF THE BIBLE ARE PEOPLE LIKE YOU AND ME WHO DISCOVERED A MERCIFUL, KIND, AND SOVEREIGN GOD.

Alcoholics Anonymous asserts that only a drunk can help a drunk. That may be true. The reason the Bible seems of so little help to many Christians is because we simply don't feel we can identify with the people in the Bible. We're "drunks," and we need a word from "drunks," not from people who will be shocked at our drunkenness. With our institutional and religious sermons, our books and our seminaries, we've made the Bible religious, and frankly, it's killing us. (And, God help me, I've been as much to blame as anybody I know.)

The Bible makes a difference in our lives not because we memorize it, teach it, and defend it. It makes a difference in our lives because the God who loved, guided, forgave, and cared for the people in the Bible when they didn't deserve it will also love, guide, forgive, and care for you and for me when it's painfully obvious that we don't deserve it either.

Now get out your Bible and read it, keeping in mind what I just told you.

THE BIBLE IS FREEING

I also feel better when I remember that the Bible is far more freeing than I thought it was.

Do you get tired of people who try to "fix" you all the time? I do, and there are a whole lot of them. You should see the thousands of letters and e-mail messages I get from people who are sure that with just a few words—written in the "love of Jesus," of course—they can straighten out my bad doctrine, make me nicer, and maybe even get me to a place where I won't cause so much damage to the church.

Just last week one of our receptionists buzzed me and said, "Steve, I hate to do this to you, but I can't find anybody else to take a call. A man on the phone is very angry. He wants to talk to you, and he's not going away until he does. Would you please talk to him? I've just about had it with him."

Being the kind and benevolent boss that I am, I picked up the phone and said in my best kind and benevolent voice, "Hi, this is Steve. Can I help you?"

"Mr. Brown," the man shouted from the phone, "there are millions of people in hell because of you."

"Cool," I said. "I didn't know I had that much power."

Evidently the man didn't share my sense of humor, because he went on to tell me that my teaching was blasphemous and doing great damage to Christians. I listened for a while and then said, "I guess this means you aren't going to send a contribution to our ministry."

He hung up.

Do you know what I felt when he hung up? I felt—and this means I'm just as neurotic as the man who called—condemned and guilty. I felt that way because I'm conditioned to feel that way. Most Christians are. We choose not to read the Bible because we already feel guilty and condemned, and we just don't need any more rules and regulations when we can't even keep the ones we know.

The Bible does have rules and regulations (they're called laws and commandments), but you'll be surprised to find out that God didn't make the rules to save us, to make us better, or even to grant us the permission to be self-righteous. (A friend of mine says self-righteous people are merely those who know the rules and can "fake it" better than those who don't.)

God gave us the rules and regulations of the Bible so we would know our need, understand our helplessness, and accept our inability to live up to them. Then—and this is why we were created—we would run to the only helper, forgiver, and redeemer around—God.

However, instead of focusing on his love, forgiveness, and kindness, we obsess on our failure to live up to all those rules and regulations. That inappropriate obsession keeps us from opening the Bible, because we already know we're sick, and we just can't stand to feel any sicker than we are.

But take heart: Jesus's angriest words were not spoken to the people who didn't live by the rules; they were spoken to those who *did*. When I remember that, I go to the Bible not with fear but with great joy—the joy of a child reading a letter from his beloved father. When a person is obsessed about his sin, he goes to a bar. When he's obsessed about God's love, he goes to the Bible.

The Puritans understood that point. (Their stern image is a myth created by people who don't know and have never read the Puritans' writings.) Consider this Puritan prayer:

*No day of my life has passed
that has not proved me guilty in thy sight.
Prayers have been uttered from a prayerless heart;
Praise has been often praiseless sound;
My best services are filthy rags.*

*All things in me call for my rejection,
All things in thee plead my acceptance.
I appeal from the throne of perfect justice
to thy throne of boundless grace.
Grant me to hear thy voice assuring me:
that by thy stripes I am healed,
that thou wast bruised for my iniquities,
that thou hast been made sin for me,
that I might be righteous in thee,*

that my grievous sins, my manifold sins, are all forgiven,
buried in the ocean of thy concealing blood.
I am guilty, but pardoned,
lost, but saved,
wandering, but found,
sinning, but cleansed.[2]

Studying the Bible didn't make the Puritans mean; it made them free.

THE BIBLE IS MORE THAN JUST A THEOLOGY BOOK

I want to share with you one more thing about the Bible. Even though just believing the Bible doesn't "settle it" for me, I do feel better when I remember that the Bible is less a theology book than I thought it was.

Donald Grey Barnhouse used to say that all of life illustrates Bible doctrine. I agree with that but would also add that all of the Bible illustrates doctrine too. In other words, the Bible isn't primarily a book about doctrine and theology.

Does the Bible teach propositional truth? Of course it does. But that's only one part of its function. Mostly the Bible is a big story encompassing many lesser stories that draw us to a God who has always revealed himself in stories. A colleague at Reformed Seminary, Richard Pratt, has written a wonderful book titled *He Gave Us Stories.*[3] God has given us stories, and when we forget that, we miss one of his great gifts to us.

Systematic biblical theology is an important discipline. Systematic theologians are scholars who take the Bible in all of its varied expressions and forms and create a system that enables us to organize, teach, and apply the "whole counsel of God" (Acts 20:27). John Calvin said of the Bible that the Old Testament interprets the New Testament, the Epistles interpret the Gospels, and the whole interprets its different parts. That's a hermeneutical principle (i.e., a principle of interpretation) that stands at the very heart of systematic biblical theology.

Truth isn't merely what works for me. It isn't whatever I say it is or whatever I decide I like. Truth is truth because God said it. We have a tendency to major on minors, to go off on tangents, to create cults, and to turn weird. Systematic theology is a helpful tool in preventing such error.

Let me ask you a question: why do we have to create a systematic theology? We have to do it because God hasn't done it. The Bible is a book that teaches us to write poetry, to tell stories, and to dance in the presence of a merciful God.

So go ahead—get the truth from the Bible. But don't forget how to dance.

A friend of mine says that belief in the Bible isn't the standard for measuring its effectiveness any more than belief in a gun is the standard for measuring its effectiveness. If someone breaks into your home and you have a .45 pistol aimed at him, even if he says he doesn't believe in guns, you wouldn't respond, "Oh, then I guess I can't use this gun. I'll have to let you rob me."

No, you'd simply pull the trigger. (Or, if you're more benevolent, you might say, "I'm getting ready to shoot the place where you're standing. If you're still standing there when I shoot, you should prepare to meet your Maker.")

The Bible doesn't need to be defended any more than God needs to be defended. I've come to see that neither God nor the

Bible needs my puny efforts to help them stand the test of truth. The Bible and God were around a long time before I got here, and they'll both do fine long after I'm gone.

I've spent too much time admiring the "gun" and defending its effectiveness.

I've decided to pull the trigger.

THERE ARE MORE THINGS IN HEAVEN AND EARTH,
HORATIO, THAN ARE DREAMT OF IN YOUR PHILOSOPHY.

SHAKESPEARE

THE BATTLE IS A LOT MORE SUPERNATURAL THAN I THOUGHT IT WAS

We do not wrestle against flesh and blood, but against the rulers, against the authorities, against the cosmic powers over this present darkness, against the spiritual forces of evil in the heavenly places.

EPHESIANS 6:12

THE PSYCHIATRIST John White, in his book *The Fight,* wrote about Christian conversion. He said that Christian conversion is like conversion to any worldview. The psychological manifestations of conversion are well known and have long been recognized and described.

Then he wrote:

> What makes Christian conversion different is that supernatural events also occur. The feeling states in non-Christian conversion are temporary. They are equally temporary in Christian conversion.
>
> But the supernatural, and often unfelt, events are permanent. They mark you in the sight of demons and angels as a human who is different. They bring your body into touch with eternity and with the Eternal God.[1]

I read those words years ago, when I was a young man. But I dismissed them. It wasn't so much that I disagreed with what Dr.

White had written, but being far from my personal experience, as I refused even to acknowledge the supernatural, it was hard to identify with his view.

I just read those words again, and like the young man who recalled his teenage years and was surprised at how much his father had learned since then, I was surprised at how profound and cogent Dr. White's words seem to me now.

The Bible is replete with evidence of the supernatural. You'll find it all in there: devils, angels, miracles, signs, wonders, magic, exorcisms, healings, prophecies, resurrections, visions, cosmic manifestations . . . and even a virgin birth. If naturalism (as opposed to supernaturalism) is your worldview, though, you'll simply dismiss all of that.

You might be surprised at how many Christians dismiss it too. I don't think very many would admit it, but they do. I know, because I was one of them.

My mentor, Fred Smith, told me once that Christians, if given the choice between spiritual power and political power, will almost always choose political power. I agree with that and would even expand on it. Given the choice between the supernatural power described in the Bible and the power of money, fame, and status, for most Christians it's a no-brainer. Money, fame, and status win every time.

We're sort of like the man in the old story who was in a flood. He scrambled onto the rooftop as the water rose. As it threatened to reach the top of his house, he cried out to God to save him. Shortly after that, a man came by in a boat and offered to take him to safety, but he said, "No, thank you anyway. I'm waiting for God to save me." Then a crudely crafted raft floated by, and he almost jumped on it. But he kept waiting for God to save him. Finally, a helicopter descended and threw him a rescue line, but he waved off the helicopter. He would rather wait for God.

The man drowned.

When he stood before God's throne, the man complained, "I trusted you, and you failed me."

"I didn't fail you," God replied. "I sent a boat, a raft, and a helicopter to save you, but you turned them all down."

That's a mildly funny story because it shows what we believe to be the narrow-mindedness of relying on the supernatural when we have the natural right at hand. And who knows? Those natural occurrences could even be God. Maybe not, but one never knows. Not only that. The story shows how really dumb it is to hold out for God's supernatural intervention when it becomes obvious that God isn't going to supernaturally intervene.

I used to think that story was funny too. Now I'm not so sure. What if the man had turned down all of the other forms of help, had trusted in God, and God really had intervened, say with a golden stepladder from heaven, an angel who performed a miracle, or perhaps a supernatural parting of the waters so the man could have climbed down from his roof and simply walked away? What if he had trusted God and there had been a definable, clear, and certain moment when God came and rescued him?

Frankly, throughout most of the "floods" in my life, I've jumped on too many boats and bailed out too quickly. That's true for most of us. But then, as the years go by, you eventually encounter something you can't fix or escape, and you begin to realize that unless God does something, all the boats in the world won't make any difference. *There just aren't that many boats, and I can't swim as well as I thought I could. If God doesn't intervene, I'm going to drown.*

Author Anne Lamott has been a guest on my talk show a couple of times. I don't agree with her about much of anything except Jesus, but that's enough. She's the real deal, and she has experienced God in a variety of wonderful events in her life. Her book *Traveling Mercies* is the record of God's actions in her life in some specific, merciful, and often supernatural ways.[2]

I once heard Lamott say that she only believed in three kinds of prayer:

First, "God, help me, and help me right now!"

Second: "Wow!"

Third: "Thank you, God."

Those are the prayers, I believe, that arise when we need—and then see—God's supernatural intervention in our lives.

IDENTIFYING THE SUPERNATURAL

And that brings me to an important principle, which is our starting point: We fail to recognize a lot of the supernatural that happens in our lives.

When we misidentify supernatural things as natural, our faith is not reinforced, and we tend to see less of the supernatural. When the supernatural is correctly identified in our lives, our faith grows—and so does the supernatural reality in our lives.

I often preach at a large church in Orlando (Northland, A Church Distributed) that features seven services (which are then multiplied, using satellite technology, in several additional locations throughout the city so that many people in many locations all worship together). When I preach the same sermon seven times between Saturday and Monday evening, a number of things happen. If the sermon is reasonably good in the first service, it gets a lot better, and by Monday night I sound like Charles Spurgeon. (Sometimes it goes so well, I want to take notes on myself!) On the other hand, if the first sermon on Saturday night is bad, I know I'm going to have a very bad weekend.

> WHEN THE SUPERNATURAL
> IS CORRECTLY IDENTIFIED
> IN OUR LIVES,
> OUR FAITH GROWS
> —AND SO DOES
> THE SUPERNATURAL
> REALITY IN OUR LIVES.

As you might imagine, preaching the same sermon that many times can produce a great deal of boredom. If you think listening to one sermon can be boring, you ought to try preaching the same one seven times. So in order to get some relief, I usually change things a bit for each service. These aren't big changes, but just enough to keep me from falling asleep during my own sermon.

Recently, when I preached at Northland, a friend of mine brought an acquaintance, whom he'd practically had to drag to the worship service. His friend was not a believer, mainly because of the hypocrisy he had encountered in the churches where he'd been involved.

My friend hadn't told me this person was coming, but for some reason, in the one service his friend attended, I started talking about the church. I said, "Whenever someone complains about the church, I want to say, 'You don't know anything. I could tell you stories that would curl your toes!' The church is a place where very human and sinful people get together. If you want to be committed to Christ and to the church, you have to be committed to hypocrisy, to bad communication, to anger, and to division. And, if you aren't willing to commit to that, don't be a part of the church."

While that comment wasn't totally irrelevant to the sermon topic, it was the only service in which I said anything even remotely like that. I had no idea why I said it or why I said it in that particular service. That is, I didn't know until my friend told me what happened as a result of those words.

His friend had been deeply touched by those words and was very close to becoming a Christian because of what I'd said. My friend thanked me. When I told him that the service his friend had attended was the only one in which I'd made that point, my friend said, "Wow. And they say there's no God."

In other words, my friend saw, experienced, and identified a supernatural work of God in that service. He could have said, "Man, what a coincidence!" He might have asked, "Wonder how that happened?" Or he could have just shrugged his shoulders and said, "Go figure."

I recall a time when that would have been my reaction. But as I've grown older, I've come to realize that the battle is so fierce and I'm so weak and sinful that what I do or don't do makes little difference. It really is God. And so, with Anne Lamott, I'm saying far more often than I used to: "Wow!"

In the parable of the talents in Matthew 25, Jesus tells a story of a master who gave one servant five talents (a talent was a measure of money), another servant two talents, and a third servant a single talent. You may remember that the first two invested the money and got a good return for their master. The third man, however, hid his one talent in the ground and then returned it to his master exactly as he had received it. The displeased master took away the one talent from the servant who had buried it and gave it to the servant who had used his original five talents and increased them to ten.

The interesting thing about that parable is the commentary on it. Jesus said, "To everyone who has will more be given, and he will have an abundance. But from the one who has not, even what he has will be taken away" (Matthew 25:29).

Many legitimate interpretations of that parable have been given; but for our purposes here, I believe the parable also applies to the principle I mentioned above. When we don't see God's supernatural hand in our lives, we'll come to see even less of his supernatural hand in our lives. When we do see it, identify it, and thank him for it, then his supernatural work increases, and we'll come to depend on it. It's like the old sermon illustration in which a young boy asks his grandfather where he sees God. His grandfather answers, "Son, I hardly ever find a place where I don't see God."

As I mentioned before, when my students express their strong (and often wrong) views on a matter of Christian importance, I often point out, "You haven't lived long enough, sinned big enough, or failed nearly enough to even have an opinion on that." (I don't say that in a critical or mean-spirited way. It's just a fact, and somebody needs to say it.)

Well, I'm not a spiritual giant or anything, but I've lived long enough and sinned big enough to see God's supernatural works in places I never expected to see them. Not only that, the years and the sin are not irrelevant to the very subject of this chapter. We'll get to that shortly.

I have some good news and some bad news: The good news is

that there is a God who will operate in amazing and supernatural ways in your life. The bad news is that you usually have to be on the rooftop without a boat, as it were, before God's supernatural work is clearly perceived.

What does it mean to be on that rooftop? And, after all these years, what have I discovered?

OUR WEAKNESS

I've discovered that I'm not nearly as gifted, as strong, or as skilled as I thought I was. I've grown less sure of what I can do and the difference I can make—and far more dependent on what God does. I don't particularly like it, but it has become necessary.

It's like the line says in "Mercy Came Running," originally recorded by Phillips, Craig, and Dean: "When I could not reach mercy, mercy came running to me." The helplessness expressed in that song is the experience of any Christian who has lived long enough and sinned big enough to know much of anything. When you haven't, the natural is sufficient. When you have, the natural is not enough. Not nearly enough.

As a young man, I was sure there was no problem I couldn't solve and no mountain I couldn't climb. My youthful self-confidence could be summed up by paraphrasing the old military slogan: the difficult I'll do now; the impossible will just take a bit longer.

In the Bible God says, "My grace is sufficient for you, for my power is made perfect in weakness" (2 Corinthians 12:9). But we don't really believe that, do we? Or, if we do, it's a theory we'd rather not test—a sort of safety net we resort to only if we get into trouble.

But something happens after you walk with Christ for a long while. As the years go by, you begin to realize that if God's grace isn't sufficient and his supernatural power doesn't work in weakness, then you don't have a chance. In other words, we don't believe the teaching of 2 Corinthians 12:9 until we have to. Then, even if we don't like it, we realize that we just don't have a choice.

I love the story of the pastor who, in his twenties, prayed, "Lord, give me the grace to win this city to Christ."

In his forties, he prayed, "Please, Lord, grant me the grace to win my church for Christ."

In his sixties, he prayed, "Lord, don't let me lose too many."

I've stood beside more deathbeds, listened to more confessions, and confronted more loss and pain in myself and in others than I ever thought possible. On those occasions I knew that I was inadequate to say or do anything that would make any real difference. I've listened to people who desperately wanted answers, and I had none. I've prayed for the sick and felt that my prayer wasn't reaching any higher than the ceiling. I've watched people I loved weep over open graves, felt intimidated by people I feared, been betrayed by people I trusted, and grieved when people I'd taught about God turned away from him.

> AS THE YEARS GO BY, YOU BEGIN TO REALIZE THAT IF GOD'S GRACE ISN'T SUFFICIENT, THEN YOU DON'T HAVE A CHANCE.

And over and over again, I've experienced a power far beyond me . . . teaching, healing, changing, comforting, strengthening, caring, loving, and empowering. The more I've seen it, the more

I've depended on it. And the older I've gotten, the more I've realized that I can depend on little else.

There's a reason for that even beyond my own weakness, and I'll tell you what it is.

OUR STRONG ENEMY

I've also discovered that the enemy is a lot more gifted, strong, and skilled than I thought he was.

Back in the days when I was an "intellectual," I couldn't bring myself, in sermons and speeches, to refer to the devil. I always referred to him as "the metaphorical personification of evil," and even then, I wasn't convinced of the reality or power of evil.

I remember one cold, dark, and rainy night on Cape Cod. A young man sat across from me in my small study—a study barely large enough to accommodate the desk and the two chairs in which we sat. He was angry. He had abused his family. He had physically attacked his employer. He had made fun of the church, of Christ, and of me. He talked about Satan in the most positive terms and God in the most negative.

Then, to my shock, he started cursing. I mean real cursing—foul, harsh, and offensive. He ended his long string of expletives with a statement that ended our conversation. "If there is a God," he said in a deep and guttural voice, "I curse him!"

I remember the hair standing up on the back of my neck and the sense of fear I felt. I had the impulse to call the police. I also remember what I thought then: "My, my, this young man is paranoid schizophrenic; he clearly needs some therapy and medication."

A few years later I visited the Philippines and a small mountain church that was packed with people. In fact, people stood all along the back and sides of that church, and the crowd spilled out into the streets. Every open window had people crowded around it.

I asked the pastor why so many had come. He told me that it was because he and the elders of the church had cast a demon out of a woman in their village after the local witch doctor had failed. He said, "Steve, this is what happens when God's power is manifest." We prayed and thanked God for his faithfulness and his supernatural power.

Between those two incidents, something had happened to me. It's called experience. Between those two events, I'd seen Satan walking down the streets of a city slum, watched him do his work with a needle dripping heroin, and seen his destructive power in the bottle clutched by a drunk sleeping it off on a bench on Boston Common. I read his handwriting on a suicide note and saw him smiling as the crowds lined up to watch an "adult" film. I saw his work in a crushed automobile, in a starving nation's desperate hunger, and in a soldier's death. Between those two incidents, I'd seen Satan in the sneer of the racist and in the lies of a politician whose only concern was power. I encountered Satan in the evils of poverty and oppression and in the death of a man who wept as he died of AIDS.

In short, between those two incidents, I grew up and realized that evil is personal, scary, and powerful. Peter wrote, "Be sober-minded; be watchful. Your adversary the devil prowls around like a roaring lion, seeking someone to devour. Resist him" (1 Peter 5:8–9).

The Bible has a lot to say about Satan. He's called a liar, the accuser, the dragon, the serpent, and the ruler of the world. Jesus prayed for Peter because "Satan demanded to have" him (Luke

22:31), and he said that religious leaders were of their "father the devil" (John 8:44). He talked about the sower whose good seeds are taken away by Satan (see Mark 4:15). Throughout the Bible the presence of the good, the pure, and the loving are juxtaposed with the presence of evil. The Bible teaches that there is a kingdom of light and a kingdom of darkness (see Colossians 1:12–14).

Here's the good news: the Bible also teaches that the battle has already been won. The Bible informs us (in Colossians 2:15 and Revelation 20:10) that the believer is playing in a ball game that's already over. It teaches that the Spirit of God in us is far greater than the spirit of Satan in the world (see 1 John 4:4) and that all we have to do is stand.

As someone has said, the dragon has been slain, but his tail still swishes. I've learned to identify the swishing of that tail. And when I see that happening, I've learned to run to the God who intervenes in a battle I'm too weak to fight—and that he has already won.

Our Choice

One other thing must be said: I've also discovered that I have a choice in my life and work. I can do it my way (the natural way), or I can do it God's way (the supernatural way). You have this choice too.

Have you heard about the pastor who played golf? After a terrible drive, an eagle picked up the man's golf ball and dropped it onto the green. Then a rabbit pushed it across the green, and finally, a beaver kicked it into the hole. "Please Lord," the pastor said, "I'd rather do it myself!"

That's the way most of us (myself included) deal with our lives.

Maybe God would intervene to help us, but then we'd owe him, and we're not into owing God. He might send us as missionaries to some third-world country with no cable television. He might even make us become preachers. So we just keep on keeping on, doing it our way, until we're so tired and have made such a mess of it that we don't have any choice but to try it his way.

When you've lived long enough and have sinned big enough, your heart turns to God more often. It's because you discovered that, if he doesn't open the door, you'll be stuck outside in the cold.

As of late, I find myself saying more often, "Help me, God—right now."

"Wow!"

"Thank you, God."

SIN IS STRONG AND FLEET OF FOOT,

OUTRUNNING EVERYTHING.

HOMER

PEOPLE ARE A LOT WORSE THAN I THOUGHT THEY WERE

*I know that nothing good dwells in me. . . . For I do not do the good
I want, but the evil I do not want is what I keep on doing.*
ROMANS 7:18–19

DON'T YOU JUST hate cynical people? I do too.

It was horrifying to me to discover that I had become one.
I called it "Christian realism," but that isn't what it was. It was
plain, old-fashioned cynicism. I often quoted Jesus's words that
we needed to be "wise as serpents and innocent as doves" (Matthew 10:16), but one day I realized that my serpent side had won
out. I had discovered that people really are a lot worse than I
thought they were. And with that discovery, something terrible
happened.

I became a cynic.

Paul wrote to the Philippians, "Whatever is true, whatever is
honorable, whatever is just, whatever is pure, whatever is lovely,
whatever is commendable, if there is any excellence, if there is
anything worthy of praise, think about these things" (Philippians
4:8). Cynicism robs you of seeing anything as true, honorable,
just, pure, lovely, commendable, excellent, and worthy of praise.
Cynicism is a hard and dark place to live.

Now I'm what you might call a recovering cynic. I still have to fight cynicism, but I'm better. I'm not better because people are, at heart, good and pure; they aren't. I'm not better because *I* am, at heart, good and pure; I'm not. I'm better because of Jesus.

Later I want to tell you what happened to make me better, but we have miles and miles to go before we get there. I could have titled this chapter "I'm a Lot Worse Than I Thought I Was," and it would have been accurate. In fact, that particular discovery was more important than my discovery about people in general, and it's one of the reasons I'm better about my cynicism. But I'm getting way ahead of myself.

THE ONE REALITY OF CYNICISM

Before we dig deeper into this, let me share with you an important truth. Cynicism and Christian realism are similar in that they both see reality. Cynicism, however, looks at only one reality.

In John 2 we're told that when Jesus was in Jerusalem, many people were impressed and believed in his name when they saw the miracles he did. Then John says that Jesus "did not entrust himself to them, because he knew all people and needed no one to bear witness about man, for he himself knew what was in man" (John 2:24–25). Jesus was a realist.

We see this realism again in Mark 3:5, when Jesus was angry at the shallowness and lack of compassion in the religious people, yet he was also "grieved at their hardness of heart."

Jesus understood that people are a lot worse than most people think they are. In fact, he understood this far better than the most hardened cynic. At the same time, though, he grieved. Perhaps one way to define Christian realism is to say that it perceives the dark side . . . and weeps. But Christian realism also goes beyond weeping; it never loses hope.

The problem with most Christians is that we have a naive belief in the goodness of people. We really believe that we're all reasonably good folks who have some stuff in us that's a bit skewed, so can't we all just get along?

Einstein is reported to have said that he wouldn't give a nickel for simplicity on this side of complexity, but that he would give his life for the simplicity on the other side of complexity. Christian realism is like that. Hope on this side of knowing the reality about the dark side of human nature isn't worth a nickel, but the hope we find on the other side of that knowledge is worth everything.

> PERHAPS ONE WAY TO DEFINE CHRISTIAN REALISM IS TO SAY THAT IT PERCEIVES THE DARK SIDE . . . AND WEEPS, BUT IT NEVER LOSES HOPE.

Our problem, I fear, is that most Christians have never faced the hard and scary side of sin—both others' sin and their own. Do you remember Jim Jones's Peoples Temple? It was a cult that started out doing good works, helping the poor, and reaching out to the disenfranchised, but it ended with the mass suicide of more than 900 people in the jungle of Jonestown, Guyana.

Deborah Layton was a member of that cult—and a survivor. In her book *Seductive Poison*, she looks back over her experience and, for the sake of her questioning daughter, tries to understand how something that started out so good could end up being so horribly evil. She wrote:

> On my own, with no one to answer to, I have kept my shame locked in a small compartment just beneath the surface. But my daughter's innocent probing has emboldened me to face the horror again, after twenty years.
>
> "Why didn't you just leave when Jim got mean?"
>
> I'm not sure. What took me so long to comprehend and finally heed the danger signs? Was it my naiveté? Perhaps it was my childlike belief in my own papa's goodness that kept me from grasping the truth . . .
>
> I'm propelled by my daughter's innocence to turn inward to my cavern of painful, frightening memories. But facing them requires that I first learn how to cope with the shame.
>
> How could we do such awful things?[1]

We all—even if the sin in our own lives is less obvious and less horrific than in that tragedy—must ask those same questions. If we don't ask them, we end up living in a fantasy world of denial.

Nothing is more dangerous than an unrealistic view of human nature. It will cause you to leave your car and your home unlocked, invest in the latest "Christian" money-making scheme, or send generous gifts to those who tell you they're trying to stand for God and save Christian values from the hordes of unbelievers bent on destroying all that's good and pure.

When we live in denial of the dark side of human nature, we get hurt needlessly, often get conned, and should never play poker. It's the difference between believing that democracy is a wonderful form of government because people are basically good and should participate in their government, and believing in democracy because people are basically bad and no one person should be entrusted with too much power. It's the difference between being genuinely surprised by evil and being genuinely surprised by good.

But coming to the discovery that people are a lot worse than I thought they were was a process.

MY THEOLOGY

It started with my theology.

The world is not a pretty place. Once I accepted that the Bible is true, I had to deal with what the Bible said about the world and about human nature. And, frankly, it's not a pretty picture.

We may like to think that people are basically good, but the Bible says that "the heart is deceitful above all things, and desperately sick; who can understand it?" (Jeremiah 17:9).

In Romans 3:10–18 Paul quoted a string of Old Testament passages that should cause us to wince:

"None is righteous, no, not one;
no one understands;
no one seeks for God.
All have turned aside; together they have become worthless;
no one does good,
not even one."
"Their throat is an open grave;
they use their tongues to deceive."
"The venom of asps is under their lips."
"Their mouth is full of curses and bitterness."

"Their feet are swift to shed blood;
   in their paths are ruin and misery,
and the way of peace they have not known."
   "There is no fear of God before their eyes."

It isn't just us; it's where we live. Although Christians have sometimes ignored biblical environmentalism, the Bible makes clear that we should act as stewards of creation and protectors of life. However, biblical environmentalism is a long way from the silly and superficial view of the environmentalist who calls earth "our mother" and worships at the altar of nature. Biblical environmentalism looks at the world the way it really is: a world in which the strongest survive and eat the weakest; a world in which earthquakes, hurricanes, and floods bring destruction and death; and a world in which very little is safe or controllable. Genesis 3:16–17 talks about the curse of the ground and the horror of pain. Paul wrote about creation being "subjected to futility," being in "bondage to decay," and "groaning together in the pains of childbirth" (Romans 8:20–22).

> THE BIBLE SAYS THAT GOD IS IN HIS HEAVEN; BUT ALL IS NOT RIGHT WITH THE WORLD, OR WITH US.

The late Christian comedian Jerry Clower used to tell a story about a wealthy farmer who, when asked, refused to donate to the local volunteer fire department. The farmer objected that, should there be a fire, his own people at the large farm would do a lot better than a bunch of volunteers.

Shortly after that, his barn caught fire. Despite the efforts of his own people, the barn continued to burn. So the farmer called the local volunteer fire department. They came in their old fire truck with its worn-out engine. With water spraying everywhere, they drove right into the burning barn and put out the fire.

The wealthy farmer was so impressed that he gave the firefighters a check for $10,000. One of the firefighters turned to the other and said, "Wow, $10,000. The first thing we're going to do is get those brakes fixed!"

It may appear, because of the thin veneer of civilization that keeps the dark side of human nature somewhat in check, that people are basically good. It can seem almost as if we even have the weather under control, because specialists can tell us what the weather will be—and after all, we have strong levies to keep out the water. It can appear that, as Robert Browning wrote, "God's in his heaven and all's right with the world." The Bible says that God is in his heaven; but all is not right with the world, or with us. Not even close.

A lot can be said about goodness in people (and we'll get to that in the next chapter), but only a shallow, unthoughtful person fails to note that our brakes, as it were, need to be fixed.

MY EXPERIENCE

The discovery that people are a lot worse than I thought they were was a process that started with my theology, but it didn't stop there.

It was also confirmed by my experience.

I didn't start out being cynical. It almost happened without my noticing it. I began with high hopes for people, for me, and for the church. I started out accepting the tenets of American optimism: that every problem had a solution, every human being wanted to be better, and every situation was redeemable.

Have you heard about the little boy who was digging in a pile of manure? Someone asked him what he was doing. The boy said, "With this much manure, there has to be a pony in there somewhere." I thought the pony was in there too. I kept digging and digging . . . only to give up in the end. You can only keep digging for so long before you at least start to suspect that the pony has long since left the scene.

Cynicism goes with the territory of being a pastor. Your heart breaks, your hopes shatter, and your mind is overwhelmed by the dark secrets of people you love. When that happens often enough, you either become a sweet, nice, and insipid clown saying things nobody believes and everybody expects, or you move into a mode of cynicism about almost everything. It's not easy to live in denial and be a pastor—at least not a sane one.

My late brother was a district attorney, and a good one. (Our father used to say that between his two sons—one was a lawyer and one was a preacher—there wasn't any problem he faced that one of them couldn't fix.) My brother once told me that in spite of the dark side of human nature he saw and the confessions he'd heard as a district attorney, he believed it wasn't even close to what I faced every day.

Someone has said that anyone who likes the law and sausage should never watch either one of them being made. I would add that anyone who likes the church should never watch how church is done. Paul wrote to his young friend Timothy that a leader of the church should never be a new Christian. I used to think that all Paul was saying was that he wanted discipline, knowledge, and maturity in the church leaders. I suppose that was a part of it. Paul pointed out the danger of a new convert becoming "puffed up with conceit" and falling "into the condemnation of the devil" (1 Timothy 3:6).

But I'm older now, and I think I better understand why Paul didn't want new Christians leading the church. More than the fear of conceit and a need for godliness drove this injunction. I believe Paul was aware that, after just one board or congregational meeting, a new Christian might be driven to become a Buddhist.

One problem seminary faculty members encounter is that students frequently go into the church unaware of its dark side. As a result, they often are hurt badly, and their ministry suffers. After discussing that particular problem at a faculty meeting a while back, we agreed that someone had to warn students and teach them how to survive the harsh reality of the church. Given that practical theology is my area of teaching, they commissioned me to do something about it.

So now, in my classes, I spend a number of lecture hours talking about how human sin is manifested in the church and how to identify and understand the dark side. I cover subjects like how to develop a "Christian mean streak," how to win the political battles without losing your salvation, how to identify "pockets of power," how not to be a weenie, how to deal with your discouragement and broken heart, and how to collect "political chips" in the poker game of church politics.

The students hate it.

In fact, often they're so irritated that they make angry comments to me. (Not an easy thing to do when a professor has the power of the grade.) They say that I'm teaching them to be manipulative and underhanded, that I'm giving them an undue negative view of the institution they will serve and the people they are supposed to love, and that I'm turning them into cynics. (Just so you know, I generally assign to one student the job of raising his or her hand when I'm so negative about the church that the students begin to think about leaving the seminary and the church altogether. When that hand goes up, I tell them about the high and holy calling of ministry, the great privilege it is to serve God's people, and stories about the people of God, their love, their faithfulness, and their kindness.)

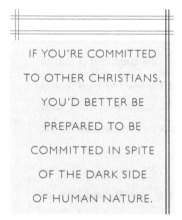

IF YOU'RE COMMITTED TO OTHER CHRISTIANS, YOU'D BETTER BE PREPARED TO BE COMMITTED IN SPITE OF THE DARK SIDE OF HUMAN NATURE.

When the students complain, I say to them, "I know . . . but you'll learn this, and I'll test you on it. One of these days, believe it or not, you will rise up and call me blessed."

And they do. I can't tell you how many times a former student has called or written to say, "Steve, do you remember how negative I was about those lectures on church politics? I repent. That stuff was better than Greek."

When you have a pastor who thinks people are wonderful, the occurrence of sin is minimal, and Christians are entirely sanctified, you've met a pastor who has never gone through a building program, offended the wealthy, stepped on the toes of an elder, preached from a text he wished wasn't in the Bible, or taken an unpopular stand. Either that, or you're dealing with a person who has lost his mind.

A pastor friend of mine founded a church and served as its pastor for more than twenty-five years. The church became a major witness to the city, and what God did there was nothing less than phenomenal. My friend finally decided to retire, and I, thinking he might need the comfort of a brother, visited him in his study.

"Next Sunday is your last Sunday, right?"

"Yes, it is, and it's going to be hard. I'm going to look out at those people, and it's going to be a struggle to keep from falling apart."

"You want some advice?"

"This would be a good time."

"Next Sunday, when you're preaching your last sermon and are about to lose it, think of someone who really ticks you off . . . someone in the church who has made your life miserable. Of course, you'll have to repent when the service is over, but it'll get you through it."

"Steve," he said, "I can't do that. I love these people. I'm their pastor. I can't think of a single person like that."

"OK," I responded as I headed for the door. "Then you're on your own. I'll be praying for you."

"Steve, wait!" he called after me, laughing. "I just thought of three."

If you're committed to other Christians, you'd better be prepared to be committed in spite of the dark side of human nature. I can't tell you the number of times people have told me that they wanted a career change because they were tired of working "in the world." They want to work in a place where their coworkers are Christians and where people love one another. "I'm tired of the struggle, the politics, and the difficulty of maintaining my witness in the secular workplace," they say. "Can you help me find a job in a Christian ministry?"

I respond in a loving and pastoral way: "Are you a fruitcake?

No place you can go is free of sin. If you like Christian organizations and the church, it's better not to work there."

If you're not a believer and have somehow picked up this book, you'll notice that I've spent a lot of time talking about us, the believers. I do so because this book will be read mostly by people who have at least a minimal commitment to Christ. Don't think for one minute, however, that I couldn't have addressed human evil among nonbelievers—and had enough material for ten books.

My Shame

People are a lot worse than I thought they were. I got that from the Bible (my theology) and from my experience. Christian realism has its anchor in both theology and experience, but it also has its personal application. When I discovered that people were a lot worse than I thought they were, I also found out that I was a lot worse than I thought I was.

It was verified by my shame.

I've told you some of the bad things about being a pastor. Now let me tell you one of the good things: I know that I'm not alone in this. Most people think that they are the only ones who are lonely, afraid, angry, doubting, and sinful. When you talk to as many people as I do, have as much contact with students as I do, and get as many letters as I do, you begin to get the feeling that we're all very human.

That's particularly true when it comes to sin.

I remember when "Sam" (not his real name) came into my office, confessing that he had stolen money from the city in which he was the city purchasing agent. It wasn't a lot of money, but if you steal ten dollars, it's no less stealing than if you'd pocketed ten thousand dollars.

Sam had lowered the price of a confiscated car that was being sold by the city. The car was priced at $600, and he marked it down to $450 so he could buy it for his daughter. No one would have ever known had it not been for a major audit of city records and the fact that Sam was thrown in with some really big-time embezzlers who had taken money from the city for years. Again, the amount wasn't what was important. My friend was guilty, and he told me so.

The next day Sam's name was in the local paper, and three or four months later, he went to trial and was convicted. He was an officer in our church, and because we had so many new Christians, I asked if we could use his story to teach them how Christians should deal with sin. (The matter is never one of *whether* Christians sin; that's a given. The only question is how we will deal with it.) "Steve," Sam said, "that would be a privilege. I would like what I've done to be of use to the Kingdom."

It's a long story, and I don't have room here to go into details. The end of the story, though, is so good that I have to share it with you. Sam resigned from the board of deacons, and during the entire process of his trial, when he was without a job and facing the horror of his shame, the entire church stood with him emotionally, financially, and spiritually.

I'll never forget the scene after Sam was (along with others) found guilty. The others held press conferences at which they proclaimed their innocence. But in the courthouse rotunda, a whole bunch of Christians surrounded Sam, placed their hands on his head, and prayed that God would be glorified through the sad episode. Many tears were shed, amid great joy that God was in charge. The day Sam was restored to the board of deacons, the entire congregation applauded.

So did the angels.

The reason I'm telling you this story is to tell you what happened the day before Sam confessed his sin to me. I was in Los Angeles and had left my car parked in the lot at my local airport. When I returned from that trip, I retrieved my car and headed to the booth where one pays the (exorbitant, I'd say) parking fees. Then, to my surprise and joy, I realized that the woman in the booth had charged me ten dollars less than I owed. I thanked her and started to drive away.

PEOPLE—MYSELF INCLUDED—REALLY ARE A LOT WORSE THAN I THOUGHT THEY WERE.

Just then I thought it would be a smart thing for me to go back and pay the right amount. I'm not altogether that pure, but being a fairly well-known preacher in our town, I was afraid she would realize what happened and know that I had cheated.

So, with great reluctance, I backed up and told the woman that I owed her some more money. She was surprised, looked again at the ticket, and then thanked me. She told me that if I had not come back, the money I failed to pay would have been taken out of her paycheck.

As Sam told me about his stealing from the city, I thought about my "almost" stealing from the city. I realized then that it could have gone either way for me—or for him.

That's a "safe" sin and one I feel comfortable telling you about. Others, though, haven't been so safe. Time and time again, people would confess their sins to me and I would think, *That could have been me.* Or, on several occasions, *I've been there and done that . . . I just haven't been caught—yet.*

To be honest, there is no sin of which I'm not capable or haven't committed. Not only that, but there are a lot of sins I would have committed if I'd had the time or was sure I wouldn't get caught.

Gradually I had become a cynic about other people; but more importantly, I became a cynic about me.

My Faith

People—myself included—really are a lot worse than I thought they were. I learned that from my theology, my experience, and my shame. But I started moving from cynicism to Christian realism because of what happened to my cynicism.

My cynicism was redeemed by my faith.

I don't want to get ahead of myself here, but I just can't leave this chapter (or you!) in the mud. When you realize that people are a lot worse than you thought they were, and when you realize that you're not above the rest of the human race, you'll have a choice to make. You can deny the reality, you can become bitter, you can run, or you can just accept the dark side as a part of what it means to be human. On the other hand, you can discover the joy, the power, and the freedom of being loved even when you don't deserve it.

Jesus really is a friend of sinners. In fact, he didn't come for the healthy but for the sick. The angel who appeared before the birth of Jesus told Joseph, "She [Mary] will bear a son, and you shall call his name Jesus [meaning 'the Lord is salvation'], for he will save his people from their sins" (Matthew 1:21).

Author Brennan Manning wrote:

The fierce mercy of Jesus is at work protecting moral failures from the fierce shaming and moral debasement of religious bureaucrats who have severed spirituality from religion, the heart from the head, and grace from nature. Real sinners deserving real punishment are gratuitously pardoned; they need only accept tenderness already present. Forgiveness has been granted; they need only the wisdom to accept it and repent. There are the ragamuffins, the poor in spirit whom Jesus declared blessed. They know how to accept a gift. "Come all you who are wiped out, confused, bewildered, lost, beat-up, scarred, scared, threatened, and depressed, and I'll enlighten your mind with wisdom and fill your heart with the tenderness that I have received from my Father." This is unconditional pardon. The sinner need only live confidently in the wisdom of tenderness.[2]

The church is not a place for people who are "together," obedient, and spiritual. If you really think it is, then you were conned. The church is actually a place for people who are needy, afraid, confused, and quite sinful. But even more important than that, the church is a place for people who have been loved . . . and have no idea why. Each congregation is, as it were, a local chapter of "Sinners Anonymous."

I have a friend, Ray Cortese, who is the pastor of one of the most dynamic and effective churches in America. It's in the small community of Lecanto, Florida, and people from all over the state attend. This man's ministry is a powerful witness to the truth of the gospel.

Ray said that when he first came to Lecanto, he thought the

community was a "sewer" where there was little concern for God, for truth, or for God's law. Ray knew he'd been sent as a prophet, so he preached powerful, prophetic sermons condemning evil and pointing to God.

Do you know what happened? Nothing. Jesus left the building.

Allow me to relay Ray's testimony and the reason he believes so many have come to his church. Ray has said, "I thought there was a sewer, and there was. It was not in the community; it was in my own heart." It was this knowledge that revolutionized his ministry, his relationships with others, and his sermons. Once he knew the truth about himself and let God love him and forgive him, Ray became a powerful voice for those who needed God but didn't think they were good enough.

The people in the church Ray serves are getting better, but they're getting better because they know that getting better isn't the point. The point is that God's power is made perfect in weakness, God's grace shines clearest through sinners, and God's message can only be heard from people who are beggars telling other beggars where they found Bread.

As I mentioned before, Alcoholics Anonymous teaches that only a drunk can help a drunk. They're right. That's why drunks get help from AA. Only people who truly understand that they're a lot worse than they thought they were can help people who are learning the same thing about themselves. Only sinners can help sinners.

People—you and I—really are a lot worse than we think we are. But as the late Jack Miller, founder of World Harvest Mission, said, "God's grace is a lot bigger than we think it is."

That's Christian realism.

THERE MAY BE SAID TO BE TWO CLASSES OF
PEOPLE IN THE WORLD: THOSE WHO
CONSTANTLY DIVIDE THE PEOPLE IN THE WORLD
INTO TWO CLASSES AND THOSE WHO DON'T.

ROBERT BENCHLEY

PEOPLE ARE A LOT BETTER THAN I THOUGHT THEY WERE

Hold fast what is good.

1 THESSALONIANS 5:21

I HAVE TROUBLE loving three people (well, there are more, but that's a different story). Let me tell you about them.

The first is a television evangelist (and you would know his name). I disagree with almost everything he teaches. In fact, he drives me nuts. I was in a supermarket parking lot recently when a little boy ran up to this man's big car. I thought the evangelist was going to drive off, but he didn't. He stopped his car, got out, knelt down, and listened to what the child had to say. In fact, when I left that parking lot some time later, he was still talking to that little boy. He was nicer than I'd expected him to be.

Don't you hate it when that happens?

The second person I have trouble loving is one of the most cynical and pagan people I know. When I want to get angry (I think better when I'm angry), I think of some sarcastic comment he made: some slur against a brother or sister in Christ or some kind of caustic and flip remark about the church.

One of the great tragedies of my life was when my younger

brother died. He was my best friend, and I miss him more than I can tell you. Shortly after that event, I ran into this man, and do you know what he said to me? He called me aside and said, "Steve, I'm so sorry about your brother's death. As you know, I don't pray much and am not even sure that God exists, but I've been praying to God for you, and I've asked him, if he exists, to comfort you." He was more compassionate than I'd expected.

Don't you hate it when that happens?

The third person is a woman who had been quite critical of me to one of my friends. I called this woman, confronting her with her alleged comments and wanting to straighten her out. Needless to say, I was angry. When she picked up the phone, I said, "Betty [not her real name], let me tell you what someone told me you said; if you did say it, we need to talk."

To my shock, "Betty" started crying. She said that I didn't need to repeat what my friend had said. "I said it," she confessed through the tears, "and I'm so sorry. I said it because of my own insecurity, and it was a terrible thing to say about you. Please forgive me, and I'll make a call and confess my lie to your friend as soon as we get off the phone." Then Betty told me about the pain she'd been dealing with and how her life had been so devastated by it. She was more vulnerable and honest than I'd thought she would be.

Don't you hate it when that happens?

Do you know why we hate to lose our enemies, the ones we've demonized? It's because we need our enemies to feel better about ourselves. We're right and they're wrong; we're good and they're bad; we're in and they're out; we know the truth and they don't.

We hate to lose our enemies because they define who we are.

And therein lies a great problem for Christians. The more we define ourselves in terms of "us and them," the greater the gap in relationships, and the more marginalized we become. Then we wonder why we're so lonely.

You've heard the old story of the uptight and condemning group of Christians who went to heaven. Saint Peter was showing some new arrivals around heaven, and they walked by a house. Peter told everyone to remain quiet and not to say a word. After they passed the house, someone asked Peter why they had to be quiet. He said, referring to the uptight and condemning Christian group, "The people in that house think they're the only ones here. It would greatly disturb their happiness and tranquility if they knew about you."

In the last chapter we talked about Christian realism. This chapter is the flip side of Christian realism: the recognition of the image of God in people, even in our enemies. People really are a lot worse than I thought they were, but they're also a lot better and more valuable than I thought too.

> THE MORE WE DEFINE OURSELVES IN TERMS OF "US AND THEM," THE GREATER THE GAP IN RELATIONSHIPS, AND THE MORE MARGINALIZED WE BECOME.

In the first chapter of the Bible, we find the story of the creation of Adam and Eve. That chapter has astounding implications for how we should view others: "God said, 'Let us make man in our image, after our likeness. And let them have dominion over the fish of the sea and over the birds of the heavens and over the livestock and over all the earth and over every creeping thing that creeps on the earth.' So God created man in his own image, in the image of God he created him; male and female he created them" (Genesis 1:26–27).

My colleague and friend Richard Pratt, in his book *Designed for Dignity*, refers to the doctrine of Adam's fall and its tragic results. (The Fall is when sin entered our world and spread like a disease, to wit the Puritan rhyme, "In Adam's fall / We sinned all.") Richard wrote about the image of God in which all human beings are created:

> How do fallen people remain the image of God? In what ways are they still God's likeness? First, people possess many basic characteristics granted to Adam and Eve in the beginning. We exhibit rational and linguistic capacities; we have moral and religious natures; we are immortal souls. Sin severely mars these aspects of our character, but it does not obliterate them. . . .
>
> Whatever else we may say about fallen humanity, we must remember that we remain the image of God. We have rebelled against our Maker, but we are still people. All of us are special creations designed with marvelous abilities and blessed with unique responsibilities in this world.[1]

A well-known song says that "people who need people are the luckiest people in the world." That may be true, but let me tell you something else that's true: people who need people and build walls to keep people out are the loneliest people in the world. For years I constructed those walls, but as of late I climbed up on a ladder and looked over the walls, sometimes even climbing down on the other side. And my life has changed as a result of that discovery.

People Are Just Like Me

I discovered that other people are just like me.

When I said that people are a lot better than I thought they were, I probably should have added that they are *sometimes* better than I thought they were. Sometimes they're worse. I'm that way too.

I remember the time, years ago, when I went with an evangelistic team into one of Boston's worst areas. It was one of those neighborhoods where white people were not supposed to go. But a number of us—both black and white—were going, and I felt I would be safe.

(I know, I know. That sounds racist, and it is. I repent.)

As a part of that evangelistic effort, we put up a screen in one of the parks and invited people to watch a film about Jesus. I don't remember the results, but what I do remember is a cacophony of feelings and perceptions. I felt fear and anxiety; if I had to die, I was glad I would die serving Jesus. By far the most salient memory I have, though, is of watching the African Americans in that community playing with their children. One father was carrying his daughter on his shoulders, and both were laughing. His daughter was the same age as my daughter, and I remember thinking, *He's just like me.*

As the film ran, I stood on a street corner adjacent to the park. I noticed a car parked there, and sitting in the car was what appeared to be a very angry black man. I thought of slavery and racism and how he probably had every right to be angry. Coward that I am, though, I started moving away from the car.

That was when this man rolled down his window and said, "Come here!"

I went. This white boy may not be the smartest you ever met, but I'm not dumb either.

"You with these people?" he asked.

"Yeah . . . ," I said hesitantly.

"Get in," he said in a gruff voice. "I want to talk to you." He reached over to the other side of the car, opened the door, and waited.

I got in, my whole life flashing before my eyes. I began thinking about my will and who would get all my stuff.

Do you know what happened? He saw my fear and started laughing. "Let me ask you a question," he said. "Do you really believe this stuff?" I allowed that I did, and he said, "Good—my life is a mess, and I want to know God. Can you help me?" Then, to my shock, he started crying.

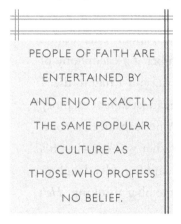

PEOPLE OF FAITH ARE ENTERTAINED BY AND ENJOY EXACTLY THE SAME POPULAR CULTURE AS THOSE WHO PROFESS NO BELIEF.

We talked for over an hour, and during that time we both shared our doubts and fears, our pain and our joys. If you'd been there, you would have seen two guys crying, holding hands, and praying together. I remember thinking about that incident after I got home. It dawned on me, with surprise, that my new friend was just like me.

That's not the only time I've discovered a common humanity in other people. I see it in my neighbors—the ones who would describe themselves as Christians and, more importantly, those who wouldn't. When we go through a hurricane (and we have gone through several together), I don't ask the guy who comes with the chainsaw whether he's a Christian. He's just a neighbor who wants to help. As we all work together, I don't gravitate toward those who are my brothers and sisters in Christ. I gravitate toward those who, like me, have a mess on their hands.

As you already know, I'm a Republican. Bill Clinton is not my favorite person in the world. I didn't vote for him and didn't agree with his policies. I remember when his mother died, though, and I saw footage of the funeral. As President Clinton brushed the tears from his eyes, I was reminded of the time my mother died and of the loss and pain I'd felt. I thought, *He feels what I felt. He's mourning the way I mourned. He misses his mother just like I do. He's just like me.* (You have no idea what it took for me to admit that.)

The other day I talked to my friend Terry Mattingly, religion columnist for the Scripps Howard News Service. He had just finished his book on popular culture, *Pop Goes Religion: Faith in Popular Culture.* He told me that every study he's seen shows that people of faith are entertained by and enjoy exactly the same popular culture as those who profess no belief.

Let me recommend a surprising book about the discovery of faith and integrity in the filmmaking capital of the world. The title is *Behind the Screen: Hollywood Insiders on Faith, Film, and Culture.* Spencer Lewerenz and Barbara Nicolosi, the editors, write in the introduction:

> Here's the situation as many see it (and if you don't think this way, you probably know plenty of people who do):
>
> Most movies and TV shows are immoral, obscene, perverted, or some combination of the three (except *7th Heaven*).
>
> Hollywood has it out for Christians in much the same way Tom had it out for Jerry or Foghorn Leghorn had it out for the dog.

The entertainment and news media are controlled by the "cultural elite," a cadre of ex-Ivy League dandies who, when not swiping manger scenes from suburban lawns, spend their time in idle cocktail chatter sneering at "conventional morality" and Costco. . . .

Blaming Hollywood has to be considered a failed tactic that needs to be abandoned.[2]

The point of that book is correct. It's easy to demonize other people as long as we can keep them at arm's length. For years I'd done that with Christians whose theology was different from mine and with unbelievers whose worldview was in opposition to mine.

So at last I looked over the walls I'd built . . . and found lonely people like me who needed a friend. I've found people who are sad, people who are funny, people who are afraid, people who are worried about paying their mortgage and about cancer. They laugh the way I laugh, at the same things I find humorous. They feel guilty the way I feel guilty and are just as insecure as I am. They bleed the way I bleed, they worry about their families the way I worry about my family, and they have moments of great courage, profound love, and graciousness—and other moments of incredible selfishness, arrogance, and self-righteousness.

In short, they are like me.

PEOPLE ARE BETTER THAN ME

But there's more: people are often better than me.

You've heard the comment, "So and so isn't a Christian, but he or she is a good person," right? While there are some theological niceties—in fact, true ones about sin and the Fall—that need to be spoken to that particular idea, the statement (at least on a human level) is true.

I want to address this subject in more detail later, but here let me say that the definition of *Christian* is not "a good person." Being "good" is not the biblical faith; it's the American folk religion.

I used to think there were two kinds of people in the world: good people and bad people. The good people were Christians, and they were in the church. The bad people were not Christians. They were not in the church. In fact, they mowed their lawns, watched television, drank beer, and went to football games on Sundays—all while the good people worshiped.

I was right about the number. There are two kinds of people. I was just wrong about who they are. There are people who are needy, sinful, and worried—and know it. And there are people who are needy, sinful, and worried—but don't know it. As I understand the Bible, the church should be made up of the people who know it.

Let me make a surprising and truthful statement with which I believe you'll agree, at least if you stop and think about it. Some of the meanest, most condemning, angriest, and hardest people I know are people who call themselves Christians. Not only that. Some of the kindest, most compassionate, and most loving people I know don't claim to have made any kind of faith commitment. In fact, you'll find both kinds of people inside and outside of faith communities.

So what's the difference? The difference is that the Christians have run to Jesus, and he's accepted and loved them. That's it. Are they getting better? Well, at least in that they know what "getting better" is. Sometimes they are better. Sometimes they're not better. And sometimes we don't know that they're better, simply because they were so bad in the first place that they had a long way to go before anybody could tell the difference. Some who ran to Jesus are better than unbelievers, and some are worse. Some are so beaten up that all they can do is be still and allow God to love them. And then there are others who've been loved long enough that they can now love others.

The difference is Jesus.

What about letting our light shine before others so they'll see our goodness and glorify God (see Matthew 5:16)? We should, of course, but goodness as defined by Jesus is quite different from what we might suppose. Usually those who are good don't know it, and others don't know it either because "Goodness" is a thing that takes place inside a person and has more to do with an attitude of love and graciousness than it does with obeying the rules. Sometimes the meanest, least godly people obey the rules. And sometimes the people of whom Jesus seems most fond have the hardest time getting it right. In the Bible, the people who obeyed the rules better than anybody else were, I would remind you, the very ones who ticked Jesus off the most.

PEOPLE NEED OTHER PEOPLE

I was quite surprised to look over my walls and find that people on the other side were often better than me. But I found out even more.

I discovered that other people need other people the way I need other people.

I smoke a pipe. (It's one of the few vices I have left. Don't write me letters or try to persuade me to stop. People more spiritual than you have already tried . . . and failed.)

Contrary to what most Christians think, there are some good things about smoking a pipe. For instance, it always gives me something to look forward to when I'm in a boring faculty meeting or listening to a boring speech. In Florida, the smoke keeps away the mosquitoes. There's more: my smoking shocks other Christians who know I love Christ but can't make the fact of my smoking fit into that image. That's probably good for them.

One other benefit of smoking a pipe is that it has made me part of a small and ever-decreasing fellowship of smokers. Everywhere I turn smokers are quitting or . . . OK . . . dying. So, as our numbers decrease, we naturally are drawn to one another outside buildings, behind barns, and in small rooms designated for those who are ugly and their mother dresses them funny (i.e., smoking areas).

You'll probably never know this if I don't tell you, but when smokers get together, they laugh a lot. They like one another and relax in each other's company. Some of my Christian friends smoke and are members of the church where I often preach. Those guys have formed a Bible study they call "Holy Smokes." They are among the most honest, authentic, and fun people I've ever met.

> I DISCOVERED THAT OTHER PEOPLE NEED OTHER PEOPLE THE WAY I NEED OTHER PEOPLE.

The fellowship of smokers is one of people who are drawn together by their sin and not by their goodness. They don't pretend to be better than they are by using mints to hide the smoky smell on their breath. They don't blush when they're together and someone sees them smoke. They hardly ever appear to be holier than thou. They're just people who need people and who gravitate to one another because of their sin.

As I peer over my walls of isolation, I find that people who are needy are drawn to one another. They take off their masks and reach out to others. The need for each other is the reason television shows about friends, companionship, and community are popular. Those programs speak to the yearning we all have to be in relationships that are more than just superficial.

So I looked over my walls to see people who are like me, people who are better than me, and people who need me as much as I need them.

WHY DO I STAY BEHIND THE WALL?

Now to a question that must be addressed before we move on: if everything I just told you is true, then why do I stay behind the wall? Or, to meddle a bit, why do you stay behind a wall? I don't know your reasons, but I know why I do it.

I stay behind the wall because I'm afraid people will learn who I am but won't accept me.

I don't want to be known.

We all wear masks.

I just finished interviewing Peter Schweizer on our talk show. He is a wonderful writer and a research fellow at the Hoover Institute. His new book is *Do As I Say (Not As I Do): Profiles in Liberal Hypocrisy*. Peter is fun to talk to, and he takes great delight in punching holes in the self-righteous balloons of both liberals and conservatives.

I opened that interview by introducing him and saying, "Peter, before we get into your book, there is something I need to say first. I'm the biggest hypocrite I know."

"Of course you are," Peter responded, laughing, "We all are. The difference is that you know it, admit it, and just announced it to your audience. The people in my book don't think they are and deny it everyplace they go."

Without making a political comment, let me say that his insight into human hypocrisy is profound. The masks we wear are many, and we wear them for a variety of reasons. Bottom line, though, is that we're afraid that if people find out what we're really like, they will reject us, criticize us, or make fun of us.

The truth is that they might love us. But let's talk about that in a minute.

Do you know what's great about being a Christian? It gives me the freedom to stop pretending. I'm climbing up the ladder and looking over the walls and even associating with those on the other side of the walls because I don't have anything to protect anymore. According to the Bible, the church is the only organization in the world where the only qualification for membership is to be unqualified. By my very membership in the church, I have proclaimed to the world that I'm a sinner, I'm needy, and I can't fix me.

If I already know that and people find out that it's true, it doesn't matter. It is a great freedom.

I also stay behind the wall because sometimes I think God wants me to stay behind the wall.

I don't want to displease God.

A misguided kind of Christianity suggests that believers

must not look at or touch anything that isn't intentionally Christian. Just as the religious people in Jesus's day were shocked that he was a friend of prostitutes, winebibbers, and sinners, so perhaps religious people today ought to be shocked that I'm friends with the same kinds of people.

> THE PEOPLE WHO SHOUT THE LOUDEST ARE OFTEN THOSE WHO ARE LEAST SURE ABOUT WHAT THEY'RE SAYING.

For about a year, when I was a teenager, I got involved in a Christian group that believed it was a dangerous sin to go to movies or to associate with people who did. I've always had a heart and a hunger for God, and when I was younger and less cynical than I am now, I listened to and believed just about anybody who spoke with authority about God. The people in that group spoke with sureness and conviction about God and what he expected of me. So, I bought it. And it almost killed me.

After that year I decided I was going to hell. I just couldn't live by the rules anymore. And I decided that if I was going to hell, I was going to have some fun doing it.

I went to a movie.

No no no. It wasn't a skin flick or a violent film. It was a Jerry Lewis and Dean Martin movie. (Now I've seen more obscene things in church than in that movie.)

During the film, though, I remembered what I'd been taught—that Jesus would return when I least expected it, and, "Do you want him to find you in sin when he returns?" I had a horrible time. I kept looking around, thinking that Jesus was coming and I was going to be in serious trouble. I knew that telling him I was there to witness wouldn't wash. And he'd never believe I'd wandered into the theater by mistake.

Then I sensed that Jesus came and sat beside me . . . and that he was laughing at me . . . and at the movie.

Since then I've learned to be very, very careful about listening to people who tell me where I shouldn't go, what I shouldn't do, what books I shouldn't read, and to what music I shouldn't listen. Instead of paying too much attention to those voices, I've decided to check out what the Bible really says. As a result, I'm a lot freer than I thought I was—and a whole lot freer than they said I was.

I am glad for this discovery, because otherwise I might never have even dared look over the wall.

Still, sometimes I stay behind the wall because I'm not completely secure in the truth I believe.

Have you ever noticed that the people who shout the loudest are often those who are least sure about what they're saying? It's like a poker game. The winners laugh and make jokes while the losers say, "Shut up. Deal and bet." When you have a winning hand, you don't have to be uptight or angry. You just enjoy the game.

Some time ago I started, and for a number of years moderated, a group called Skeptics Forum. The ministry consisted of a weekly meeting of atheists, agnostics, and all sorts of nonbelievers. Only one Christian was allowed to attend the meetings, and that was me. The purpose of the forum was to provide honest answers to honest questions from nonbelievers.

Do you know my initial feelings when I began the Skeptics Forum? I was scared spitless. I had nightmares in which these learned nonbelievers destroyed my faith. I was sure they would have me for lunch. I thought I would probably make a fool of myself, bring shame on Christ, and destroy his kingdom with my shallow and insufficient answers.

What really happened was just the opposite: many of the people who joined the forum eventually became Christians, and the others stopped laughing.

The point is this: the genuine can be tested. Truth is truth, and a good place to see if the truth will stand up under questioning is among people who don't believe it. You may be surprised at how well the truth holds up. Once I discovered that, it was easier to climb over the wall.

Finally, I stay behind the wall because I'm afraid of love.

Love brings with it obligation, and frankly, I'm already more obligated than I can handle.

In honest and authentic relationships, you climb over the wall. You start talking. You discover that these aren't half-bad people. The truth is, you kind of enjoy being with them. You begin to realize that they like you and you like them.

That's when you notice their tears—and you find that you care.

It can be uncomfortable to love. It's messy, and it puts you in a position of obligation. But not to love is dangerous. Oh, you may not get hurt or disappointed. And it feels safe on this side of the wall, even if it is boring. The problem, however, is that once you start building walls, it's hard to stop. One day you'll wake up to discover you're closed in by those walls you built. You'll have just four walls and only a little room. You'll find that without intending to, you've become hard, angry, and very lonely.

Jesus saw the tears of those on the other side of the wall. He knew what his love for them would cost—and he chose to love anyway.

Then he told us to do what he had done, and he promised that if we did, he would always go with us.

OF ALL MARVELOUS THINGS, PERHAPS THERE IS NOTHING
THAT ANGELS BEHOLD WITH SUCH
SUPREME ASTONISHMENT AS A PROUD MAN.

CHARLES CALEB COLTON

SELF-RIGHTEOUSNESS IS A LOT MORE DANGEROUS THAN I THOUGHT IT WAS

Do nothing from rivalry or conceit, but in humility
count others more significant than yourselves.
PHILIPPIANS 2:3

I JUST BOUGHT a new Honda Accord.

I guess I started thinking about it when the producer of our radio program, Erik Guzman, bought an old car and converted it to run on cooking oil. He was quite pleased and, I might say, a bit self-righteous. He could go to McDonald's for a burger and fries and fill up his fuel tank at the same time. The problem was that his car smelled like French fries. Whenever I followed him in traffic, I got hungry. His car also put out a lot of pollution. While it may be better to smell French fries than gasoline fumes, the smoke from either is unpleasant.

Still, the more I thought about it, the more I thought I should do something for myself and for the world.

So I bought the Honda Accord. It isn't just an Accord. It's a hybrid Accord.

The combination gasoline and electric engine is a little more expensive, but I didn't mind. I was willing to pay more because I care. I care about the environment, and I care about the quality of life. I'm concerned that people who don't care are buying gas-guzzlers with engines that pollute the atmosphere and kill the trees.

I don't want to sound overly harsh, but too many people don't care. They drive their big cars, and they're killing all of us. Every time I see someone in an SUV, I want to shout, "You cretin! Don't you care about the earth? Don't you care about our air? Don't you care about our children?"

I've even thought about printing cards to place under the windshield wipers of such cars: "Please save our children. Get a hybrid!"

There, I've said it, and it felt really good.

Of course, I get a tax write-off for buying the hybrid, I save money on gasoline, and the hybrid isn't tested enough to be sure that the batteries won't explode and ruin an entire forest. Doesn't matter that I could have bought a cheaper car and given what I saved to missions or that a lot of people can't afford a car at all.

> WHEN WE START THINKING ABOUT IT, WE BEGIN TO REALIZE THAT SELF-RIGHTEOUSNESS IS PERHAPS THE MOST DANGEROUS OF ALL HUMAN SINS.

I feel good about myself and my environmentally friendly decision. That's what's important. Perhaps I was even able to make you feel guilty. It hardly gets any better than that, right?

In Luke 18 Jesus tells a story about self-righteousness. The story has two characters: a religious man and a horrible sinner—a dishonest tax collector. Jesus said that the religious man came to the temple to pray, looked down at the sinner, and then prayed, "God, I thank you that I am not like other men, extortioners, unjust, adulterers, or even like this tax collector. I fast twice a week; I give tithes of all that I get" (Luke 18:11–12).

The tax collector's prayer was considerably shorter. Jesus said that he wouldn't even look up when he prayed, "God, be merciful to me, a sinner" (Luke 18:13).

Jesus explained that the tax collector found favor in God's eyes (i.e., was justified); the religious man didn't. Then Jesus made an astounding statement. He said, "Everyone who exalts himself will be humbled, but the one who humbles himself will be exalted" (Luke 18:14).

Let's talk about self-righteousness. I only recently found out that I was an expert. You may not know it, but you probably are too. I'm not trying to put down or demean anyone. I'm simply stating a conclusion that's hard to avoid when we think about it. And when we start thinking about it, we begin to realize that self-righteousness is perhaps the most dangerous of all human sins.

In its religious form, self-righteousness is a conviction that one is better than others, morally, spiritually, or theologically. Yet the word has come to connote something more than that: it is the spurious view that one is not like other people. Self-righteous people always think they speak as outsiders. The religious man opened his prayer with an interesting statement: "God, I thank you that I am not like other men" (Luke 18:11).

I didn't always think of self-righteousness as altogether that dangerous. But it is. Let me tell you why, and why it doesn't seem so.

CHAPTER 8
SELF-RIGHTEOUSNESS IS SUBTLE

First, self-righteousness doesn't seem dangerous because it's quite subtle.

I never thought I was self-righteous. In fact, the more self-righteous I became, the less self-righteous I thought I was. Being a religious professional, especially if you have any success at it, can be dangerous in this respect. I know. The churches I served all grew, the books I wrote sold, and the invitations to speak were so numerous that I couldn't even accept a small portion of them. And then there was radio and television. I was, of course, doing it all for God. When others criticized me, I was kind but rather cool. After all, I knew I was God's servant doing God's work, and doing it with a degree of excellence that gave me the sense that I was OK and others weren't.

Paul wrote, "Let anyone who thinks that he stands take heed lest he fall" (1 Corinthians 10:12). I never underlined that verse because I never thought I had to underline it. That's the very nature of self-righteousness: it's a disease that can hardly ever be diagnosed by the person who has it.

I'd like to tell you that I'm cured, but I'm not even close. I am, however, beginning to realize that when I die, I'm not going to even leave a hole—that God doesn't *need* me, and that my sin is so great that I need to be very careful in talking about anyone else's. It took a near nervous breakdown, acute embarrassment, and some honest brothers who forced me to look at myself for me to become the spiritual giant now writing this book. (And if you believe that last part, you need help as much as I need to repent for writing it.)

Let me tell you about my friend Rusty Anderson. Rusty died in an automobile accident a few years ago, and I miss him more than I can express. He and I had been friends for twenty-five years, and in that time we had come to trust each other with our secrets. Rusty loved me and I loved him, and in the context of that love, we spoke truth to each other.

I was once offered a position as president of a prominent educational institution. A number of people I respected told me they were sure I was the man God had called to that place.

Before I tell the rest of this story, there's something you need to know. I ran away from kindergarten, and school was a struggle for the next twenty years. Frankly, it seems to me insane that I'm teaching in a graduate school of theology with people who have their doctorates from places like Oxford, Harvard, Cambridge, and Duke, when I'm not even a nurse.

I remember my brother Ron on his first day of school. Our mother asked him how he liked it, and Ron said that it was OK, but he wasn't going back. When she told him that he didn't have a choice, he cried. I was older than he was and found that funny—but I understood.

Back to the story.

Some well-known and discerning people decided that I should be the president of this academic institution. At first I thought they had lost their minds, but then I started thinking perhaps they were more discerning than I'd first believed. Perhaps I knew more than I thought I knew. Perhaps I had become such an example of integrity, morality, and purity that I was the right person for the job. Perhaps my humility had blinded me to my own insight, my own depth, and all the knowledge I'd acquired over the years. I moved from surprise to consideration and was quickly moving up to a coronation when Rusty called.

I don't even know how he found out where I was or that I'd been offered the position. Maybe God told him. I was in a hotel room in another city, getting ready to speak at a conference when he called. Rusty didn't even say hello or ask me how the conference was going. "Who do you think you are?" he almost shouted over the phone. "Are you nuts? You can't do this. You will fail at it, embarrass yourself and your family, and destroy the place."

Shortly after Rusty's somewhat less-than-kind call, I phoned the people on the committee and told them to find somebody else.

Self-righteousness is so subtle that sometimes someone who loves you has to step in and tell you the truth.

Are you an obedient Christian, a respected leader, an esteemed expert—and know it? That can be the most dangerous thing in your life right now. If you've failed, been dishonored, or are in sin—and know it—right now, that might just be the best thing you have going for you.

SELF-RIGHTEOUSNESS IS INCREMENTAL

Self-righteousness is also dangerous because it's incremental. It never starts out as self-righteousness; it starts out as something fine and good.

My friends and colleagues Charlie and Ruth Jones (of the ministry Peculiar People) are among the finest and most gifted dramatists I've ever seen. They are a part of the Key Life team when we do Born Free seminars (a seminar on radical grace, infectious joy, and surprising faithfulness) and The Great American

Medicine Show (a fun evening during which grace and freedom are demonstrated, and people don't bring Bibles).

One of their dramatic sketches touches on the story Jesus told in Luke 18 to which I referred above. Their sketch, however, has a twist to it that is profound. The religious man prays his prayer, and the tax collector asks for mercy; then, immediately after that justifying prayer, the forgiven sinner stands up and shouts, "Thank God, I'm a Christian and I'm free!"

Then, during the remainder of the sketch, the new Christian encounters a variety of people who—while mildly pleased with his new status as a believer—try to teach and disciple him. One tells him that it's fine that he's saved but that he isn't really saved until he speaks in tongues. Another recommends the study of Reformed theology. One woman shows him how he should get up in the morning and have devotions. And it goes on and on until that new Christian is burdened down with all it "means" to be a Christian.

> IF YOU'VE FAILED, BEEN DISHONORED, OR ARE IN SIN—AND KNOW IT—RIGHT NOW, THAT MIGHT JUST BE THE BEST THING YOU HAVE GOING FOR YOU.

In the final scene the new Christian enters a church to pray and opens with these words: "Lord, I thank you that I'm not like other men. I get up at four in the morning to have devotions, I speak in tongues, I read theology, I . . ." And the sketch ends.

That is precisely the way it happens. I know. I've lived there a long time. The sin of self-righteousness is always built on the foundation of the good and the pure. The man in Jesus's story really had done all the things he said he had done. He tithed, and he fasted twice a week. He was an honest and just man. He did not commit adultery. And yet he was not justified in God's sight. If that doesn't scare you, self-righteousness has blinded you.

It does me sometimes.

SELF-RIGHTEOUSNESS IS ADDICTIVE

I am simply amazed at what I will do to appear to be better than others. I suspect it may be one of the reasons I do what I do for a living. When you're a pastor, a seminary professor, or a Bible teacher, people think of you as spiritually a cut above others. I, of course, deny any such assertion. Then people tell me they're impressed with my humility. That makes me feel good, and then I want to fake being even more humble. It's a vicious cycle.

Why do you think the religious man in Jesus's story stood so tall while the tax collector only looked at the ground? It was because the religious man not only *felt* he was more righteous than others, but he also wanted everyone to see him and to *know* he was more righteous than others. The tax collector didn't want anybody to notice his level of righteousness.

The nature of self-righteousness is that it is never a private sin. Most people know (even if they don't admit it to themselves) what they're really like. Jesus warned about practicing one's righteousness in public (Matthew 6:2–6):

When you give to the needy, sound no trumpet before you, as the hypocrites do in the synagogues and in the streets, that they may be praised by others. Truly, I say to you, they have received their reward. But when you give to the needy, do not let your left hand know what your right hand is doing, so that your giving may be in secret. And your Father who sees in secret will reward you.

And when you pray, you must not be like the hypocrites. For they love to stand and pray in the synagogues and at the street corners, that they may be seen by others. Truly, I say to you, they have received their reward. But when you pray, go into your room and shut the door and pray to your Father who is in secret. And your Father who sees in secret will reward you.

This morning I went by our local doughnut shop. As I'm writing this, I'm having coffee and a doughnut. Well, I probably should tell the truth. I've had more than one doughnut.

I ate six. OK?

I honestly didn't mean to eat that many doughnuts. I bought the half dozen so I could share them, but nobody came into my study. (It is a fairly safe bet that no one else in the office gets here this early, so maybe there was a volitional element in my eating all of the doughnuts.) I thought I'd have just another one. Before I knew it, the box was empty. I couldn't believe I'd eaten them all.

Do you know why I ate all of the doughnuts? I ate them because I like doughnuts, and the more I eat them, the more I like them. In fact, after I finish this paragraph, I may go back to the doughnut shop and get some more so I can share them with others when they come in later this morning. I might even have one or two more myself.

Jesus talked about the reward for people who give to the needy so others will notice or who pray so others will see. Reward is the stuff of which addictions are made. The more one is rewarded, the more one will do that which brought the reward.

It's called positive reinforcement. Once you get a lot of praise for your beauty, your spirituality, your academic ability, or your righteousness, that praise can become habit forming—and then, in your addiction, you will do almost anything to get more.

People will sell their souls in order to receive praise. I've been there—and still visit on occasion.

SELF-RIGHTEOUSNESS IS INDISCRIMINATE

If you're not religious, you may be intrigued by what I've said about religious folks. Perhaps you're saying to yourself, *Yeah! They're a bunch of hypocrites, and I always knew it.*

Do you know what you just did? You just manifested a self-righteousness that is equal to and perhaps greater than the religious self-righteousness about which I've written.

Once we see how pervasive self-righteousness is, we begin to see it everywhere—in ourselves and almost everywhere else. I challenge you to start observing the world where you live from the perspective of what we've considered in this chapter. You'll be amazed. Instead of seeing politics in terms of left and right, religion in terms of God haters and God lovers, environmentalism in terms of those who love and those who hate the environment, look for the self-righteousness. Instead of seeing issues, look for the ego.

A friend of mine is a consultant to major industry. I asked him how he knew what to do and how to find problems. He said, "I always look for the ego."

Don't define everything in terms of wicked capitalists and naive socialists, those who are at war with Christmas and those who are trying to preserve our best traditions, or those who believe the Bible and those who don't. Not even in terms of those who stand for God, motherhood, and justice and those who don't. Look for the ego.

In whatever issue being addressed, you'll usually find that the self-righteous quotient is far higher than the concern quotient. You will find criticism of Christian fundamentalists by people whose secular fundamentalism dwarfs the fundamentalism of the people being criticized. Political correctness and the attendant feelings of self-righteousness have their equivalent in religious communities with religious correctness. If you look at victims (the ones who talk the most about justice), you'll find self-righteousness. On the other side, if you look at the people who wield power, they do it with the self-righteous notion that they know better, understand more, and are more informed than others.

> IN WHATEVER ISSUE BEING ADDRESSED, YOU'LL USUALLY FIND THAT THE SELF-RIGHTEOUS QUOTIENT IS FAR HIGHER THAN THE CONCERN QUOTIENT.

And if you look hard enough, you'll find self-righteousness in what I just wrote.

Arrogance, condescension, disdain, contemptuousness, aloofness, and pomposity are everywhere. You'll find it in the good guys, in the bad guys, and in those you think are good guys and bad guys. It's in the religious and the nonreligious. You can find it on both sides of every political and social issue. You'll find it in Washington, in Hollywood, and in your own town.

And if you look hard enough, you'll find it in what I just wrote.

Self-righteousness is so subtle, so incremental, and so addictive that most folks don't see it in others or in themselves. Once you get it, though, you simply can't get away from it.

My wife, Anna, just read what I wrote above. She said, "That's true except for our dogs, Annie and Thor." She's right. It's in everybody but Thor and Annie. Well, everybody but Thor. Annie is a bit self-righteous with Thor.

Before we look at some ways to fix self-righteousness, let me say one more thing.

SELF-RIGHTEOUSNESS IS DESTRUCTIVE

Self-righteousness makes genuine love almost impossible. My friend Fred Smith says it's impossible to love anybody who has sinned unless you're aware that you are capable of the same sin. Self-righteousness, then—believing ourselves better than others—makes it almost impossible to love, and thus destroys relationships.

One of the most effective prison ministries I know of is Riverside House in Miami. My friend Cleve Bell is an incredible force for good inside the prison system. Prisoners love him because he loves them.

I've often accompanied Cleve and watched him minister to prisoners. Cleve is a great communicator, but that isn't why he's great with prisoners. He's an exciting musician, but that isn't the reason for his effectiveness. He runs an administratively tight ship at Riverside House and at the halfway house it operates, but that's not why Cleve has success with prisoners.

Cleve is good at what he does because he found Christ when he was in prison. Cleve was convicted of first-degree murder, so when he talks to prisoners, he's pretty sure they haven't done anything he's not capable of doing—or has done. Prisoners listen because Cleve loves them, and he can love them because he knows the truth about himself.

Do you ever wonder why Christians are ineffective in evangelistic efforts? It's because most people who aren't believers think of us as angry, condemning, uptight, and judgmental. (I know, I know; they are too, but that isn't the issue. We're talking about us.) Do you know why they think that? Because it is—God help us—a lot truer than most of us would like to admit. And the reason we are that way is because of self-righteousness.

In Calvin Miller's wonderful book *The Singer*, he has woven in statements (outside the movement of the story) that are like little bursts of light. Let me share one of them with you:

> Institutions have a poor safety record. The guillotines of orthodoxy keep a clean blade that is always honed for heresy. And somewhere near the place where witches die an unseen sign is posted whose invisible letters clearly read:
>
> *WE ARE PROUD TO REPORT 0 WORKING DAYS*
> *LOST TO INJURY OR ACCIDENT.*
>
> *—THE MANAGEMENT*
>
> Let us pray.[1]

We destroy people with our guillotines of self-righteousness.

Perhaps more important than what self-righteousness does to relationships and to the church is what self-righteousness does to our personal relationship with God. The first thing a sane person feels when standing before a holy, righteous, and sovereign God should be extreme humility. If we don't feel that way, we've been worshiping an idol.

In fact, if you're a Christian and can take communion, can worship and be involved in ministry without wondering why in the world God would forgive, love, and save you, you simply haven't understood the gospel.

It must be hard to be a king, to have won many battles and have people singing your praises, without becoming self-righteous. Ask David. Don't ask him when he's doing fine and wielding power; ask him after his fall—his acts of adultery and murder. This is a hard lesson, but an important one, and maybe even worth the pain: "The sacrifices of God are a broken spirit; a broken and contrite heart, O God, you will not despise" (Psalm 51:17).

I sometimes tell my students a story about a young, arrogant preacher who climbed into the pulpit with his "peacock feathers flying in the breeze." The sermon was a colossal failure, and the young man was devastated. As he walked down from the pulpit, tears of shame filled his eyes. An old saint standing at the foot of the stairs said, not unkindly, "Son, if you had entered the pulpit the way you left it, you might have left the pulpit the way you entered it."

That principle holds true when we enter the throne room of a holy God too.

WHAT'S THE SOLUTION?

I have no idea.

I suppose we could have no convictions, never be obedient, and fail at everything we do. That, however, violates everything

I know about what God would have us be. He wants us to have strong convictions, to be obedient, and to reach for excellence.

I used to counsel single people who wanted to be married that they should place that desire on the altar and give it up to the Lord. When they had sacrificed the desire, perhaps God would give the gift of marriage to them.

My friend Genevieve Caldwell, whose book *First Person, Singular* dealt with the topic of singleness, heard about the advice I was giving. She said, "Steve, I love you, but I just heard what you've been telling single people. That's the dumbest thing I've ever heard. You're telling them that they should relinquish their God-given desire to be married, and when they get to the point where they don't want it anymore, God will give it to them. That's crazy!"

It was crazy—about as crazy as rejecting the gifts God has given you, setting aside the convictions that have come from him, and deliberately failing at the tasks to which he has called you, and then hoping God will give them back to you when you don't want them any longer.

I guess we could pretend we don't have those convictions and those gifts. But that's even crazier than trying to get rid of them. There's already enough pretending, and besides, if you've read this far, you probably can see that we'd only become self-righteous about what we pretend: "Hey, everybody, look at me. You know I'm beautiful, gifted, and bright, but I'm pretending I'm not, and you should praise me for that."

So, what to do? I don't know. I wish I did. I wish I could give you a formula or a ten-step program to deal with self-righteousness. But there is no system. I wish I could teach you a prayer that would fix it. No prayer like that exists, that I know of. I wish I could tell you how to be really, really humble. But I don't know how.

Wait.

Maybe that *is* the solution. Maybe the solution isn't in anything we *do* but rather in what we *know*. Could it be that the solution isn't in making ourselves less self-righteous but rather in recognizing that we *are* self-righteous?

In fact, the secret to getting better might be to simply recognize how difficult it is to get better, take our self-righteous shortcomings to Jesus, and tell everybody we know that we've been to him—and why we went there.

Oh, and by the way . . . God said I could keep the hybrid if I quit talking about it.

WICKED MEN OBEY FROM FEAR;

GOOD MEN, FROM LOVE.

Aristotle

Obedience Is a Lot More Difficult Than I Thought It Was

*Truly, I say to you, the tax collectors and the prostitutes
go into the kingdom of God before you.*

MATTHEW 21:31

Is IT RELATIVELY easy for you to be obedient to God and his commandments? If it is, then you can skip this chapter. In fact, go right on to the next one.

I'll wait while you do.

Okay, now that it's just us sinners, can we talk?

When I was younger, I bought into the philosophy that the world was getting better and better, in every way, every day—and that most people were too. And even if they weren't, Christians certainly were. It was called sanctification (i.e., the process whereby a believer, by God's grace and the work of the Holy Spirit, gets better and better), and it was promised by God. Paul said that what God begins in my life, he'll be sure to complete (see Philippians 1:6).

I still believe that. It's just a lot harder than I thought it would be.

That's bad. Well, sort of, but it isn't as bad as you might think. I know I'm supposed to get better, and I know that God would have me be his obedient and holy child. I also know that I'm not even close.

If you know much about my ministry and what we teach at Key Life, you know that our purpose is to get you and those you love Home with radical freedom, infectious joy, and surprising faithfulness to Christ. The operative words there are *radical, infectious*, and *surprising*. I often teach that your sin can be the best thing in your life—*if you're aware of it*; and your obedience can be the greatest danger in your life—*if you're too aware of it*. Having read the material in the previous chapter, you know that's true because of the horrible danger of self-righteousness.

Now I want to take that teaching a bit further. I want to do something that may surprise you and will almost certainly offend you. Stay with me, though, because what I'm going to say now is the essence of the gospel and, frankly, a lot more helpful than religion. I want to say a good word about sin.

What? A good word about sin?

Yes, but I'm not the first one to do that. Martin Luther once wrote a letter to George Spalatin, a Christian brother who had worked with Luther during the Reformation. Spalatin had a difficult time dealing with overwhelming feelings of guilt over some spurious advice he'd once given. When Luther learned of Spalatin's condition, he wrote to him the following:

> My faithful request and admonition is that you join our company and associate with us, who are real, great, and hardboiled sinners. You must by no means make Christ to seem paltry and trifling to us, as though He could be our Helper only when we want to be rid from imaginary, nominal, and

childish sins. No, no! That would not be good for us. He must rather be a Savior and Redeemer from real, great, grievous, and damnable transgressions and iniquities, yea, from the very greatest and most shocking sins; to be brief, from all sins added together in a grand total. . . .

Dr. Staupitz comforted me on a certain occasion when I was a patient in the same hospital and suffering the same affliction as you, by addressing me thus: Aha! you want to be a painted sinner and, accordingly, expect to have in Christ a painted Savior. You will have to get used to the belief that Christ is a real Savior and you a real sinner. For God is neither jesting nor dealing in imaginary affairs, but He was greatly and most assuredly in earnest when He sent His own Son into the world and sacrificed Him for our sakes.[1]

I like to sin. If I didn't like to sin, I wouldn't sin. In fact, one of the most difficult things I do as a Christian leader is try to persuade people not to do what they obviously would like to do. When the bank robber was asked why he robbed banks, he said, "Because that's where the money is." Duh. Sin is attractive, and we sin because we like it.

Other than that (and that only sounds positive), though, there are some positive things one could say about sin.

Knowing God

If it weren't for sin, I would never have known God.

When Luther made his oft-quoted comment to the effect that one who sins ought to "sin boldly," he was not saying that sin is a good thing but rather that Jesus was a bold Savior. If your sin is small, the savior who saves you will be rather small. In fact, your small savior will not be Jesus but a substitute. After all, you won't need the real thing.

However, the intensity of a problem can be measured by the intensity of the solution. In other words, the bigger the problem, the bigger its solution must be. If our sins had been little and our needs small, God could have sent a book. But he sent his Son. That ought to give us some idea of how big the problem is. As I pointed out before, when Jesus's disciples were asked why he spent so much time with sinners, Jesus explained that he was a physician and had come for the "sick" people—not for those who were well (see Matthew 9:10–13).

> THE INTENSITY OF A PROBLEM CAN BE MEASURED BY THE INTENSITY OF THE SOLUTION.

Let me tell you about my lawyer friend John Longino. He moved to the mountains of north Georgia to escape the fast track he'd been on in Miami. John had been on the fast track because he's good at what he does. For a number of years, John was the corporate attorney for some major companies and was much in demand as a trial lawyer. He finally made enough money to move to the mountains, and that's where he is now.

John is smart, gifted, articulate, and mean . . . really mean. Don't get me wrong—he loves Jesus. In fact, in the national park near his home, John often takes doughnuts and coffee to the campers on Sunday mornings and leads a worship service for them. If you first saw John doing that, you'd be surprised to see him in court. There John doesn't seem at all the same nice, mild-mannered, spiritual person who would conduct a worship service in the woods. When John is in court, he's one of the most effective advocates I've ever seen.

At Key Life we've owned a certain 800 number (1-800-KEY LIFE) for several years. It's a long story, and I'll spare you the details, but while two other companies (which we had once hired to collect order information from calls to that number) were in litigation, one of them stole our number. That's right, they just took it, turned it off, and closed it down.

I tried to talk to AT&T about getting the number back, but they said (firmly but nicely) that we had lost it, and their policy was not to make a number available again for six months. Even then, we would simply be one among others who wanted that number. That meant that Key Life was in serious trouble: we get thousands of calls each month through that number.

So I called John, and he went to work.

John eventually found out the name and private phone number of the corporate attorney at AT&T. "I'm getting ready to bring the mother of all lawsuits against you guys," John told the attorney. "And not only that; I'm going to make a ton of money doing it. However, I work for these crazy Christians in Florida, and they say I have to talk to you before I sue."

That afternoon AT&T gave us back the number.

I could tell you a bunch of stories about John and about his kindness to me. One time, as we sat on his front porch in the mountains, John said, "Brown, I love for you to get into trouble." I asked him why, and he said, "I love you, and the only time I see you is when you're in trouble."

Jesus says sort of the same thing to me. Did you ever think that grace (i.e., God's unmerited favor) is attracted to sin? That's what the apostle Paul said: "The law came in to increase the trespass, but where sin increased, grace abounded all the more" (Romans 5:20). In other words, if it weren't for my sin, I never would have known Jesus. And while I hate my sin, seeing it makes me thankful for my closest friend and my King, Jesus Christ. If not for my sin, I never would have known him.

LOVING OTHERS

If it weren't for sin, I never would have loved you, and you never would have loved me.

Well, you probably don't know me, and I probably don't know you; but if we knew each other, the only way we could love each other would be because of our sin.

Do you remember when Jesus washed his disciples' feet (John 13)? During his last supper with them, to their astonishment, Jesus took a towel and did what only servants were called to do: he washed the guests' dirty feet. As he did, he talked about being made clean. Then, when he had finished, Jesus said something important:

> Do you understand what I have done to you? You call me Teacher and Lord, and you are right, for so I am. If I then, your Lord and Teacher, have washed your feet, you also ought to wash one another's feet. For I have given you an example, that you also should do just as I have done to you. Truly, truly, I say to you, a servant is not greater than his master, nor is a messenger greater than the one who sent him. (John 13:12–16)

The dean of our seminary chapel, Reggie Kidd, decided to devote one of the weekly services to a foot-washing ceremony. When he told me about it, I said something spiritual, like, "I'll participate in that kind of service when a hot place freezes over! Hope you guys have a really good service. I won't be there."

I'm driven by guilt, though. As the day approached, I decided I ought to go. I carefully washed my feet that morning and put on clean socks, and I went. Do you know what happened? It was one of the most emotionally moving and profound worship services I've ever attended. You have no idea what faculty washing each other's feet and faculty washing students' feet does to a professor. You have no idea what students washing each other's feet or students washing faculty members' feet does to a student. At the end of the service, we all came down to the front of that big chapel and held hands while we sang:

> Amazing Grace! how sweet the sound,
> That saved a wretch like me!
> I once was lost, but now am found,
> Was blind, but now I see.

Why did Jesus wash his disciples' feet? They were dirty (a metaphor for sin). Why did Jesus tell us to wash one another's feet? They are dirty. In the context of our human contact, who washes dirty feet? People with dirty feet wash the dirty feet of others. Therein is the profound truth about sin: Love in response to goodness, perfection, and obedience isn't love; it's a reward. Only those who don't deserve it can be loved, and only those who have been loved can love.

Discovering Joy

If it weren't for sin, I never would have discovered joy.

Earlier I referred to a Luther quote on sinning boldly. Now

let me give you the entire quote. Luther wrote to his friend and colleague Philipp Melanchthon, "God does not save people who are only fictitious sinners. Be a sinner and sin boldly but believe and rejoice in Christ even more boldly for he is victorious over sin, death, and the world."[2]

> IF NOT FOR MY SIN, I NEVER WOULD HAVE COME TO KNOW JESUS . . . OR LOVE OTHERS . . . OR EXPERIENCE THE JOY AND RELEASE OF ACCEPTANCE.

I asked a friend how he was this morning, and he responded, "I'm doing so good that I think God has overlooked me. I think if he had not overlooked me, I would have been dead from the lightning bolt he would have thrown at me." My friend then told me that he never wanted to be like Job, about whom God said to Satan, "Have you seen my servant Job?"—and then some very bad things happened. "Steve, I want to be obedient and stuff, but not that obedient. I prefer God to overlook me."

Then my friend said, "But he hasn't overlooked me, has he? He has even numbered the hairs on my head, and he continues to bless me, to be fond of me, and to forgive me. Go figure."

He's got it, and "it" is the source of true joy. I don't care what you say about me, how much you dislike me, or whether you want to be with me, because I have a Friend who is quite fond of me. Of course, that fondness is the result of the Cross; nevertheless, it's genuine and a source of great joy.

Jesus said that the kingdom of heaven is like "treasure hidden in a field, which a man found and covered up. Then in his *joy* he goes and sells all that he has and buys that field" (Matthew 13:44, emphasis added). If it weren't for my sin, I never would have known the joy, the release, and the pleasure of knowing that I'm accepted and acceptable—no matter what I've done, no matter where I've been.

Do you remember where Jesus found you? I remember where he found me. I was living in an apartment near Boston where, from my front porch, I could see the bay on my left and the ocean on my right. I remember the money I made and the beautiful wife God had given me. I remember the baby (our first) we were expecting. I also remember standing on that porch and crying like a baby. I was miserable, empty, lonely, and sinful. And my life had little meaning.

Then Jesus came. Just thinking about where I was when he found me is a source of great joy. If not for my sin, I never would have come to know him . . . or love others . . . or experience the joy and release of acceptance.

HATING SIN

I don't want to go too far down this road without also saying that, not only am I thankful for my sin, but I also hate my sin. My friend Tony Campolo is a regular on our talk show. We call him our "go-to liberal"—and he is that, at least politically. Tony is also one of the most compassionate and unconditionally loving people I've ever met. Tony, as you may know, was a friend of Bill Clinton's (who probably wouldn't be my best friend), and he has reached out to the gay community with love and without compromising the truth of what the Bible says (which is something I'm not sure I could do).

Last week Tony was on our show as we discussed televangelist Jim Bakker. Shortly after Bakker had been exposed for some sinful behavior, Tony had preached a sermon titled "I Am Jim Bakker." Tony's wife, Peggy, told me then that she wished Tony hadn't done that, because "everybody now thinks he's messing around."

On our show I mentioned what Peggy had said, and Tony responded with something I've thought about ever since: "Steve, do you know how people say that one should love the sinner and hate the sin? That's not what my Bible says. My Bible says that we should love the sinner and hate our own sin."

I agree with Tony. I gave you an "argument for sin." But that's not all: I hate my sin. I really do. I'm not a good person, and I've given you sufficient evidence of that in this book. However, you probably don't know many people who want to please God more than I want to please him. When I thought my sin would make God angry, I was rebellious and angry with him. But when I found out how much he loves me, I was drawn to that love. In the light of his love, I see things about myself that embarrass me, that offend me, and that cause me to cringe. I'm not good, but I want to be.

OBEDIENCE AND HOW TO GET THERE

And that brings me to the main question: If obedience is so hard, how can we be obedient? How can we get better?

In the previous chapter, on self-righteousness, I ended with a suggestion for becoming less self-righteous—for how to get better. That truth is a powerful weapon against all of our sin and disobedience: the secret to getting better might be to simply recognize how difficult it is to get better, to go to Jesus with it, and to tell everybody we know that we've been to him and why we went there.

One of the most radical passages in the entire Bible is found in Luke 7. In that chapter Luke tells about a dinner party Jesus attended. It took place at the house of Simon, a Pharisee—a very religious and good person. I suppose the people at the dinner were all religious and good people like Simon. The dinner party was interrupted by a commotion—a prostitute had "crashed" the party because she wanted to see Jesus. Jesus treated her with kindness: he did not condemn her but rather forgave her sins and then held her up as an example of love.

For those of us who want to get better but are finding out how difficult that really is, this story is instructive. If you haven't yet discovered how difficult obedience is, then you haven't tried very hard to be obedient. I've walked with Jesus for a long time now, and sometimes (not all the time, or even most of the time, but sometimes) I find myself following closely in his footsteps. When I do, though, it isn't for the reasons you may think.

Let's consider some things Luke's story reveals about the prostitute's going to Jesus, about Jesus's response, and about what these things mean for us.

The prostitute in the story knew she was a sinner and ran to Jesus. Yet when we know we're sinners, too often the last place we want to go is to him.

Luke says "a woman who had lived a sinful life brought an alabaster flask of ointment, and standing behind him at his feet, weeping, she began to wet his feet with her tears and wiped them with the hair of her head and kissed his feet and anointed them with the ointment" (Luke 7:37–38). This woman risked embarrassment, ridicule, and condemnation because she saw something about Jesus that most of us forget: he welcomes sinners.

A lot of people have given us a terrible misrepresentation of God. Parents use him to scare children into obedience ("I may not see you, but God sees you!"). We use his anger at and hatred of sin to gain power and to manipulate others. We speak of God as a "consuming fire"—and that's true—but we forget to tell the rest of the story. We self-righteously talk about hell with an attitude of, "You'll get yours, and I'm glad!"

But don't forget that the Word (which was God) "became flesh and dwelt among us . . . full of grace and truth" (John 1:14). If you forget that, trying to be obedient will kill you.

At the risk of repeating myself over and over again, remember that even if you never get any better, God won't love you any less than he does right now. And even if you get a lot better, God won't love you any more than he does right now. But if you don't understand that, you'll never get better, because only those who know that God will love them even if they don't get better will ever get any better.

The prostitute didn't go to Jesus to get better; she went to Jesus to be loved by the one man who would love her unconditionally—without wanting anything from her in return.

The prostitute not only knew that she was a sinner and ran to Jesus, but she didn't care who noticed. And we care way too much.

One of the interesting things about this incident is that Jesus seems almost to have wanted to embarrass the prostitute. A kinder man, we suppose, would have excused himself and gone outside to talk with the woman. A more compassionate man, we suppose, would have talked to her in private and would have helped her. That's not what Jesus did. He pointed her out. In fact, Jesus turned to his host, Simon, and asked, "Do you see this woman?" (Luke 7:44).

What's with that?

I think Jesus pointed out the prostitute because he knew she wouldn't mind being pointed out. One of the most surprising things about the whole episode is the fact that she would crash a Pharisee's dinner party at all. I don't know about you, but if I were a prostitute, the last party I would want to attend would be one at the house of the chairman of the board of deacons.

If you were sleeping with your girlfriend, no longer liked her, and wanted to sleep with someone else, to whom would you go for advice, Dr. Laura (Schlessinger)? You'd have to be crazy. I don't know if you've ever heard her popular talk show, but I can't listen when someone like that calls her. I want to say to the caller, "Are you out of your mind? She's going to kill you." As you may know, Dr. Laura af-

> ONLY THOSE WHO KNOW THAT GOD WILL LOVE THEM EVEN IF THEY DON'T GET BETTER WILL EVER GET ANY BETTER.

firms traditional and biblical values, clearly calls for responsibility, does not abide idiots easily, and will call it like it is—as in, "You're a self-absorbed cretin who's thinking of nobody but yourself!"

For most of us, this prostitute's going to Jesus would seem like a promiscuous and arrogant teenager going to Dr. Laura. But that's not the case. The prostitute wasn't arrogant. She was a moral failure, her life was a mess, and Jesus was all that mattered.

In Don Miller's wonderful book *Blue Like Jazz*, he tells of some Christian students on a secular campus who set up a confessional booth at a college fair. No, they weren't taking confessions . . . they were giving them. When a student came into the booth, wondering what in the world was going on, he or she was asked to sit down in the confessional chair. Then the Christians confessed their sins to the person in the chair![3]

That's so astounding and so good that I can hardly stand it. It may also point to a major secret to obedience: being authentic about our own sin. When we care too much about what other people think, we start pretending we're something they might like. And when we pretend too much, we end up discovering that it's almost impossible to become what we fake.

In chapter eight we talked about the tax collector in Jesus's story who wouldn't even look up and could only pray, "God, be merciful to me, a sinner!" (Luke 18:13). We saw that the repentant tax collector was justified in God's eyes. Now let me tell you something else that happened. By way of commentary on his story, Jesus said, "Everyone who exalts himself will be humbled, but the one who humbles himself will be exalted" (Luke 18:14).

What does that mean? It means that authenticity and honesty (as in confession without caring who knows) is a source of great help in our efforts to be obedient. James wrote, "Confess your sins to one another and pray for one another, that you may be healed" (James 5:16). The great and important supernatural principle is this: honesty about who we are makes us better than we are. After all, the Holy Spirit's power, like a stream, only runs downhill.

So, if you've discovered that obedience is more difficult than you thought it would be, go tell someone. Tell him or her who you really are, what you've really done, and how often you've been disobedient. You'll be embarrassed. But you'll be better too.

Jesus didn't tell the prostitute in the story to get better. Yet we think that's all he does.

If you're really religious, then you're not going to like what Jesus said next: "'Her sins, which are many, are forgiven—for she loved much. But he who is forgiven little, loves little.' And he said to her, 'Your sins are forgiven.' Then those who were at table with him began to say among themselves, 'Who is this, who even forgives sins?' And he said to the woman, 'Your faith has saved you; go in peace'" (Luke 7:47–50).

Go in peace?! What about discipleship, joining a good synagogue, and studying the Scriptures? What about obedience?

Listen: Jesus didn't tell the prostitute to be better, because he didn't have to tell her to be better. Her sin was not the issue; her love for Jesus was the only issue. Jesus knew she would walk the walk, or at least walk it better than she had before.

Christians are too often obsessed with sin. You know it's true. An outsider would think that it's all we care about—being pure and holy. If an unbeliever is asked about what we do, he or she will probably say something like, "Those Christians are miserable and won't be happy until everyone else is miserable too." And they may have a point. I remember a man telling me, after I had talked to him about Christ, "No thanks! I'm already guilty enough—I don't need any more guilt."

The truth is, almost everything of any importance is found while looking for something else. You can't chase peace, love, or happiness. Those things result from pursuing, or in relation to, something else. The same is true with obedience. I've decided to accept the fact that obedience is harder than I thought it was, and because it is, it's going to be slow in coming. I don't like it, but it's true. So if I can't get better quickly, then what am I to do?

I'm going to Jesus. I'm going to him because he doesn't care how I come. My purity, my goodness, and my obedience aren't the issues. My guilt, I believe, has only one purpose, and that isn't to make me better; it's to send me to him, the only one who loves me, forgives me, and will accept me no matter where I've been, what I've done, or where I'm going.

One other thing about this story—it's a side road, but it's important nonetheless:

I believe Simon became a follower of Jesus because of the prostitute.

Simon had a question, but he never asked it: "When the Pharisee who had invited him saw this, he *said to himself,* 'If this man were a prophet, he would have known who and what sort of woman this is who is touching him, for she is a sinner'" (Luke 7:39, emphasis added). Then notice the next words: "And *Jesus answering said to him . . .*" (Luke 7:40, emphasis added).

Do you see it? Simon never asked his question aloud, and yet Jesus answered it. How do you think we know Simon asked that question if he never voiced it? Where did we get that detail of the story if no one ever heard Simon's question?

From only one person: Simon. I submit that the only possible reason Simon would have talked about it would be as a part of his testimony about Jesus. I can see him, months after that incident, telling his friends—perhaps during a worship service in the early church or in some kind of public forum—"Hey, let me tell you about Jesus. One time when he was at my house for dinner, he read my mind. Is Jesus great or what?"

Obedience really is more difficult than I thought it was. But God's grace is a lot bigger than I thought it was too. Again, the secret to getting better is simply to recognize how difficult it is to get better, go to Jesus with it, and tell everybody we know that we've been to him and why we went there.

When we do that, not only do we get better . . . everybody else does too.

LOVE IS INDESTRUCTIBLE;
ITS HOLY FLAME FOREVER BURNETH;
FROM HEAVEN IT CAME,
TO HEAVEN RETURNETH.

ROBERT SOUTHEY

LOVE IS A LOT STRONGER THAN I THOUGHT IT WAS

Above all, keep loving one another earnestly,
since love covers a multitude of sins.

1 PETER 4:8

A NUMBER OF years ago I spoke at a conference in a rather large convention center. I was the preacher/teacher for the plenary sessions in the auditorium, and running concurrently in another part of the center was a conference for young people whose parents were attending the larger conference. The teacher for the youth conference was a prominent professor. He was (and is) a brilliant scholar, a profound thinker, and a much-respected Christian leader . . . but, frankly, in spite of all his gifts, he had no business leading a conference for teenagers.

When I first learned that this man would lead the youth conference, I wondered who had invited him and what they were smoking when they did. I thought, *Those teenagers are going to eat him alive!* I didn't believe there was any way he'd make it through the week.

I often tell youth pastors and parents of teenagers that, if they die while doing either, they get a free pass to heaven. In fact, they won't even be asked about Jesus when they get to heaven. The angels will just say, "You poor dear, you come right on in." It's a joke, of course, but people laugh because they know that teenagers are a tough audience. The teens at this conference were not the "nice" ones who operate the rides at Disney World or who usher on Youth Sunday in your church. These were teenagers with black fingernails, purple hair, rings in funny places, and clothes that have been designed to keep adults away.

Anyone who speaks at a teen conference had better be charismatic and exciting. And I don't want to be unkind, but this man was anything but charismatic and exciting. In a contest of which was most exciting, listening to this man speak or watching paint dry, watching paint dry would win every time.

Anyway, on the final day of the conference, everybody—teenagers and adults—came together to talk about the event, to praise God for what he had done, and to pray together. Some nice things were said about me during that final session, but what was said about this dull and boring professor was "over the top." A steady parade of teenagers got up and talked about how God had touched their lives, about what their conference leader had taught them, and about what was going to be different when they returned home. Many of them wept as they told how this man had deeply affected them.

The next year both this professor and I were invited back to speak at that same conference. I determined to find out his secret for working with teenagers. So toward the end of the conference, when I was on a break, I sat at the back of the youth auditorium, watched, and listened. The man was as dull as I thought he would be—pedantic, boring, and long-winded. I had just about decided that there was no accounting for taste and got up to leave when something happened that I'll never forget.

This professor began to cry. In the middle of his presentation, he got emotional and lost it. And when it happened, he turned his back on his audience. (That's *not* a good communication technique.) With his back to the teenagers, the professor took out his handkerchief and wiped the tears from his eyes. I noticed that while this professor wept, there wasn't a single smart comment, no derision, no snickers. It was as quiet as a tomb—the kind of quietness that suggests awe.

When the professor pulled himself together, he turned back to face the teenagers, and this is what he said:

"I'm so very sorry. I hate it when I do that.

"I've been spending a lot of time with you young people. I've been listening. You've been kind enough to tell me your secrets, to confess your sins, and to describe the hard places in your lives. It's a great privilege and honor that you would trust me with that. As I promised, I've been praying for you and thinking about you a lot.

"And, no, I'm not going to tell anybody what you told me . . . as long as you're nice to me."

Everybody laughed.

The man continued: "But just then, while I was teaching, I couldn't think about what I was teaching; I started thinking about you. I hate for this conference to come to an end, not because I like conferences, but because of you. You've gotten under my skin and into my heart, and I will continue to think about you and pray for you long after this conference is over. I want you to know that I love you, and deeply.

"But I don't love you nearly as much as God loves you. Try to remember that."

That was it! That was his secret. Love trumped power, charismatic speaking, authority, and skill. Love trumped everything else.

It always does, you know.

I didn't know for sure what it was that I was witnessing then. That conference happened a lot of years ago, but even then I knew I'd seen something authentic and powerful, maybe even supernatural. I saw tears I didn't expect and power I couldn't explain.

LOVE TRUMPED POWER, CHARISMATIC SPEAKING, AUTHORITY, AND SKILL.

I had seen a profound love—both human and supernatural. I might have been able to name it then, but I didn't understand it. I understand it better now . . . because I've been loved longer. A degree of wisdom comes with long and enduring love. Love sees things the mind can miss.

One of the great love stories of history is that of Martin Luther and Katharina Von Bora. As a monk, Luther had pledged not to marry. The more he studied, the more Luther realized that marriage was a gift from God . . . but only for others. Certainly not for himself.

When Luther finally did decide to marry, it was not for love. He wrote to a friend, "The rumor of my marriage is correct. I cannot deny my father the hope of progeny, and I had to confirm my teaching at a time when many are so timid."[1] Luther married to confirm his teaching, to irritate his adversaries, and to give his parents grandchildren. Those aren't the most romantic reasons for marriage, and it's surprising that Katharina (or any other woman, for that matter) would have him, with a mindset like that.

But Katharina loved Luther, and in time Luther found the wonder of love in the arms of his "beloved Katie." He wrote, "I would not exchange my Katie for Paris or all of France, for Venice or all of Italy, for God has given her to me and has given me to her. . . . There is no sweeter union."[2]

It took me a long time to discover that love is a lot stronger than I thought it was. I was so busy practicing my religion, getting my theology right, teaching the truth, and working for God that I almost missed love.

I Incorrectly Defined Love

I almost missed love because I didn't understand what it was.

I suspect you've heard the often-quoted words of C. S. Lewis on the various forms of love.[3] Lewis wrote about four Greek words for love, each meaning something slightly different (*storge*—affection, *philia*—friendship, *eros*—romantic love, and *agape*—charity). Lewis explained that agape love is from God. Without it, the other kinds of love become distorted.

In 1 Corinthians 13 Paul wrote that agape love is patient, kind, and without envy or boastfulness. It isn't arrogant or rude, and it doesn't insist on its own way. Love isn't irritable or resentful, and it rejoices in truth. Love, Paul went on to say, bears, believes, hopes, and endures all things . . . and it lasts forever.

I find Lewis's comments on love helpful, and I'm moved by Paul's great chapter on love. I've often taught on the "concept" of love, defining it in terms of what I had learned. The problem with propositional truth about love, though, is that it's not love. It's like the difference between reading a book on lions and meeting one, or between looking at an advertisement for Florida oranges and eating one.

The song says we're "looking for love in all the wrong places." I suppose there's some truth to that, but it would be more correct to say that we fail to see love in those "wrong places." Love is everywhere, but we can easily miss it. You have to have experienced the real thing before you can see it in the "wrong places." As with the professor I described at that conference, love was there—but I missed it.

I once saw love in a prostitute's weeping for another prostitute who had been abused by a client. I watched love as a gay man nursed his partner, who was dying of AIDS. A friend of mine told me about love when he went to bars because that's where his friends were, and he felt more comfortable there than in church. You can find love in a cult where doctrines are wrong and at a party where drunks are cursing. You can find love in a racist as he watches his child being born. You can find love in a Muslim mosque where a father weeps for his son, who just blew himself up thinking he was doing it for God. I've seen love in a liberal church that was feeding the poor and in a fundamentalist church that forgave and restored a sinful preacher.

Sometimes love is masked by harshness, lust, and booze; but if you know where to look, you can find it. Love hangs out in brothels, churches, bars, and missions. Love is in the homes of the rich and of the poor, in the smoke-filled back rooms of the powerful, as well as the smoke-filled back rooms of the unpowerful. Love is sometimes emotional and sometimes unemotional. Love is sometimes harsh and sometimes gentle. Love can be a mighty river or

a gentle stream; but mostly, love hangs out in the "wrong" places
... or else it isn't love.

What matters isn't *where* you go to find love; it's what you're looking for. It's not really the wrong place that causes you to miss love but the wrong definition. It's not what's in your head but what's in your heart.

If you can't define it with the experience of your heart, you can miss love. I know.

Love Is Subtle

I almost missed love because love is quite subtle.

Hosea is one of the great love books in the Bible. It's the story of how Hosea—a religious professional—is called to marry a prostitute by the name of Gomer. Needless to say, that's not the best career move for a preacher. (Just try introducing that new wife to the deacons or the Ladies Aid Society at your church.) But Hosea was an obedient servant of God and did what God called him to do. He married Gomer. Three children were born into that marriage.

Then she left.

I guess Gomer remembered the "good times," the parties, and the gifts. For whatever reason, she left her husband and went back to her old life. Hosea was devastated. I can only imagine he was in the process of healing when God came to him a second time. God told Hosea to go back into the red-light district of the city to find his wife, who, having hit some hard times, had sold herself into slavery. God instructed Hosea to bring Gomer back home and to love her. And Hosea was obedient to God.

As I mentioned in chapter four, Donald Barnhouse, great

Philadelphia preacher of another generation, used to say that all of life illustrates Bible doctrine. He wasn't the first preacher to understand that. Hosea understood it as well and used his experience to illustrate an incredible truth about a God who loves those who are unlovely. God loved the "prostitute" (his unfaithful people) with a love that would never let go—even though, like Gomer, they certainly didn't deserve it. Consider Hosea's wonderful description, a powerful image of subtle love: "When Israel was a child, I loved him, and out of Egypt I called my son. The more they were called, the more they went away; they kept sacrificing to the Baals and burning offerings to idols. Yet it was I who taught Ephraim to walk; I took them up by their arms, but they did not know that I healed them" (Hosea 11:1–3).

> LOVE IS GOD QUIETLY TOUCHING A WORLD THAT IS FILLED WITH HATRED, ENVY, AND DEATH—BY TAKING ON HUMAN FLESH AND DWELLING AMONG US.

They didn't know?

That's the nature of love. When love comes with power and authority—with flags waving and swords swinging—it isn't love. Love never chases, it woos. Love never demands, it requests. Love never shouts, it whispers. That's why love is so easy to miss.

I have a problem with the Christmas holiday. And, no, it isn't because of the commercialism, the "pagans'" war against it, or Christ's being taken out of it. I have no quarrel with merchants making a living and being able to pay their employees. I don't mind unbelievers enjoying Christmas. I don't expect them to put Christ in Christmas. I love the gigantic and impressive Christmas spectaculars and the performances of Handel's *Messiah*. When the

"Hallelujah Chorus" is sung, I stand because I can't help it. I love the Christmas sermons and the decorated churches.

What really worries me is that the love that came down at Christmas was much quieter and more subtle than all that. I think Christmas bothers me because it's too loud, too clear, and too manipulative. Love is far more subtle than that.

"God so loved the world," the Bible says, "that he gave his only Son" (John 3:16). Love revealed itself in a stable and completed itself on crossbeams between two thieves. Love came to a small town and to a people who were conquered and weak. Love is easy to miss because love is not a thing; it's a person. Love is God quietly touching a world that is filled with hatred, envy, and death—by taking on human flesh and dwelling among us.

Jesus said, "Greater love has no one than this, that someone lays down his life for his friends. You are my friends. . . . No longer do I call you servants, for the servant does not know what his master is doing; but I have called you friends" (John 15:13–15).

We all live in the "wrong places." After all, it's the only place we can live. And love is there, but it's not until you've been loved by God that you see it.

But I'm getting ahead of myself.

I Didn't Think I Needed Love

I also almost missed love because I didn't think I needed it.

Paul said that a person who's doing fine should be careful, because it's easy to fall (see 1 Corinthians 10:12). I did fine for only so long before the wheels came off my wagon.

The world in which we live is extremely dangerous. (More to come on that in the next chapter.) It's unforgiving, uncaring, and harsh. We encounter so much pain, death, and sin in the world that sometimes I can hardly stand it. The world is far more dangerous than I thought it was when I was young.

Forgive me if I sound glib. I'm not trying to provide answers to the problem of pain and evil. I've already told you that I don't have the answers. But I do know one of them. The world in which we live is the only kind of world where, when it gets dark enough, you can see the light. It's the kind of world that will cause you to look for something better. The prayer that falls from the lips of those who have felt pain, been brushed by death, and struggled with sin is both honest and powerful: "God, the ocean is so very big. My boat is so very small. Have mercy on me."

When my father was dying, his physician said to him, "Mr. Brown, you have about three months to live. We're going to pray, and then I'm going to tell you something more important than what I just told you." They prayed, and then my father's doctor told him about Jesus and Jesus's love.

I almost missed the experience of love because I was doing fine, thank you very much. It was only when I was no longer doing fine—when my sin had almost overwhelmed me and when I grew sick of the lies and the pretense, realizing just how truly helpless I was—that I found love. Or, perhaps, love found me. When it did, I realized I had always known there ought to be a God like that somewhere.

I Thought I Had to Earn Love

I almost missed love because, once I knew I needed it, I thought I had to earn it.

Love, if it's earned, is not love; it's reward. Love, in order to be love, must be directed toward one who is unlovely. The Bible says,

"While we were still weak, at the right time Christ died for the ungodly. For one will scarcely die for a righteous person—though perhaps for a good person one would dare even to die—but God shows his love for us in that while we were still sinners, Christ died for us" (Romans 5:6–8).

Everything we know about the world suggests that if we work hard enough, we'll be rewarded. In school we did our homework, studied for tests, and were attentive . . . and got good grades. At work, if we perform well, we get bonuses, compliments, and promotions. As children, if we were nice, we got praised; and when we weren't nice, we got punished.

I know, I know. It doesn't always work that way, and things aren't always fair. But we all know that it ought to work that way, and more often than not it does. The golfer knows that, while practice may not make perfect, it does make him better. The hardworking teacher, doctor, or lawyer knows the rewards of that hard work.

It stands to reason, then, that God's rewards are given to those who work hard at being obedient, religious, and pure. Right?

No! That lie is from the pit of hell and smells like smoke. Therein is the reason so many miss God's love. As I mentioned before, the church is the one organization in the world where the only qualification for membership is not being qualified. The less qualified you are, the more qualified you become.

Now, that's crazy. And it would make us more comfortable if God got it right. In fact, the church—God have mercy on us—has been working hard at trying to remedy God's error. Jesus came for the sick . . . but if you get well, he'll like you a whole lot more. Jesus came for the sinners . . . but if you want to be blessed by

God's love, repent of your sin and get rid of it. Jesus came for the outcasts, the rebels, and the lost . . . but we, in our effort to fix God's mistake, turn them away.

In teaching my seminary students how to preach, I start by exposing a number of religious myths for what they are—myths. The biggest myth is that they shouldn't preach sermons they aren't living. In other words, they have to walk the talk. A preacher *should* be a model of love and grace, no question about it. A leader in the church *should* be following Christ. But if a preacher only preaches what he lives, then his sermons will be very short—and he'll only preach once or twice a year.

Even more importantly, that preacher will give credence to the lie that God had more than one perfect preacher. And he'll fail to communicate the most important and difficult truth of the Christian faith. As preacher Paul put it, "The saying is trustworthy and deserving of full acceptance, that Christ Jesus came into the world to save sinners, of whom I am the foremost" (1 Timothy 1:15).

My friend Jack Miller taught that the most repentant person in the congregation ought to be the preacher. In fact, without repentance, there is no power in what is taught. That point is profound, because anything less suggests that if one is good enough, one can be loved by God.

I believed that lie for a long time. I still struggle with it. But when I believe that lie, I miss the incredible and unconditional love of God.

LOVE IS STRONG

One other thing must be said: Love sometimes appears weak because it's so subtle that it whispers, and because people keep trying to earn it and therefore never experience it. But love is not weak; love is a lot stronger than you think it is.

Paul wrote that three things will last forever: "Faith, hope, and love abide, these three; but the greatest of these is love" (1 Corinthians 13:13).

Love is incredibly strong because once you experience it, you can never "un-experience" it. You cannot stop love, and you cannot keep it from re-creating itself in you.

John the apostle wrote, "We have come to know and to believe the love that God has for us. God is love, and whoever abides in love abides in God, and God abides in him. By this is love perfected with us, so that we may have confidence for the day of judgment" (1 John 4:16–17).

> LOVE IS INCREDIBLY STRONG BECAUSE ONCE YOU EXPERIENCE IT, YOU CAN NEVER "UN-EXPERIENCE" IT.

Paul wrote that when God starts something in the life of the believer, he will bring it to completion (see Philippians 1:6). What that means is this: what God begins, he always completes; so just the fact of its beginning is the absolute promise of its completion. That, of course, includes love. Paul also said that the love of Christ controlled him (see 2 Corinthians 5:14).

When John wrote about the incarnation of God in Christ, he said, "In him was life, and the life was the light of men. The light shines in the darkness, and the darkness has not overcome it" (John 1:4–5). "No one has ever seen God; the only God, who is at the Father's side, he has made him known" (John 1:18). And John is the one who told us that "God is love" (1 John 4:16).

At the coming of Christ, love was let loose in the world . . .

and nobody can stop it. God—the awesome and sovereign creator and sustainer of all that is—is love. God is not loving; he *is* love. God does not act in a loving way; he *is* love. God is not sometimes loving and sometimes not; he *is* love. The darkness has no reality of its own; it is only defined in terms of the absence of light. The Light has come, and everything that is dark will be destroyed in its wake.

Someone has said that as long as there are exams, there will be prayer in public schools. That's true, but let me tell you something else that's true: as long as there are sinful people who want to be forgiven, marginalized people who want to be accepted, frightened people who want hope, anxious people who want peace, and dying people who want life, there will be love—God's love, available to those in need.

I once heard a preacher say to a group of people, who were not altogether happy about his being there, that he loved them.

"Yeah, what do you want from us?" a man called out from the back row.

"I don't want anything from you. I have everything I need. I just want you to know that I'm going to be your friend even if you don't want me to be your friend, and I'm going to love you even if you don't want me to love you."

The people were quiet. What do you say in the face of that kind of love?

That's the message God has given to those who will receive it.

God has also called those who know him to that same message—to live and to give in love. Only those who have been loved can love, and their love is measured by the degree of the love with which they have been loved. And here's what we know about God's love for us: "I am sure that neither death nor life, nor angels nor rulers, nor things present nor things to come, nor powers, nor height nor depth, nor anything else in all creation, will be able to separate us from the love of God in Christ Jesus our Lord" (Romans 8:38–39).

You can't stop love.

THE UNREST OF THIS WEARY WORLD IS
ITS UNVOICED CRY AFTER GOD.

THEODORE T. MUNGER

THE WORLD IS A LOT MORE DANGEROUS THAN I THOUGHT IT WAS

I am sending you out as sheep in the midst of wolves,
so be wise as serpents and innocent as doves.

MATTHEW 10:16

MONDAY MORNING IS often depressing for me. But it's not depressing because I have to go to work.

It's depressing because I have to pray.

At Key Life we keep a list of people who have written, called, or e-mailed us, asking us to pray for their needs . . . and that list is updated every Monday. A number of staff and volunteers pray, and I'm one of them.

The list is quite long (often a couple hundred items), and it simply gives the first name of the person who requested prayer and a short statement about the need. Let me share with you some of the items on this morning's list:

. . . just discovered lung cancer; doctor doesn't give much hope

. . . husband whose wife left him and their three small children

. . . sexually abused

... husband has been unfaithful and says he doesn't love her

... her baby just died, and she can't go on

... trying to deal with drug and alcohol addiction

... soldier in Iraq asks prayers for his wife and three children back home

... mother is dying

... just been diagnosed with MS

... pastor whose ministry has been destroyed by his sin

... single mother who lost her job

... was raped and is trying to deal with the pain and shame

... son has not spoken to him in more than four years (trying reconciliation)

... husband is in hospital and dying ... no place to turn

... son died in Afghanistan

... arrested, and the charges are false

... lost his home in the hurricane

... living in fear and can't sleep

... that her son will allow her to see her grandchildren

... dealing with divorce

... homeless couple with small child

... wife committed suicide

It goes on and on. By the time I finish praying, I'm depressed.

Did you read about the Romanian prisoner, Pavel M, who

filed a paper to sue God for crimes against his person? He claimed that his baptism was a pact he made with God in which God pledged to protect him. God had not followed through with his side of the bargain, so Pavel brought suit.

We, of course, would not file suit against God. That's silly. Whom are you going to get for a lawyer, and how will you get God to show up for the trial? But I can understand Pavel. I might try a lawsuit too if I knew God wouldn't strike me dead.

I have a book in my library that promises those who read it a way to have a "victorious and abundant life." That makes me wince, and it also makes me wonder where in the world the author has been living. I hope he reads this chapter. The fact is, a "victorious Christian life" is sometimes no more than keeping your nose above water. The fact is, the "abundant Christian life" is sometimes no more than getting by without messing it up so badly that it can't be fixed.

> A "VICTORIOUS CHRISTIAN LIFE" IS SOMETIMES NO MORE THAN KEEPING YOUR NOSE ABOVE WATER.

Sometimes we forget that we aren't Home yet. When we forget that fact, our expectations far exceed what God has promised. I'm afraid that honest unbelievers wonder about us: they think we may have lost our minds. It's quite clear to anybody who cares to observe that Christians are sometimes in great pain, have doubts, wonder about meaning, and suffer about the same as everybody else.

What thinking Christian has not wondered with the psalmist why God treats so well those who aren't even God's friends? "For the wicked boasts of the desires of his soul, and the one greedy for gain curses and renounces the LORD. In the pride of his face the wicked does not seek him; all his thoughts are, 'There is no God.' His ways prosper at all times" (Psalm 10:3–5). And what thinking Christian doesn't affirm Saint Teresa and her humorous but profound comment, "Lord, you would have more friends if you treated the ones you had a little better"?

Today, the day I write this chapter, I interviewed Dr. David Downing, author of *Into the Wardrobe: C. S. Lewis and the Narnia Chronicles*, on our talk show. He also has written several other books about Lewis, including an award-winning biography, *The Most Reluctant Convert*.

When I asked Downing why he was so enamored with C. S. Lewis, he explained that had been raised in a kind but very strict home, and when he got to college, he began to have doubts about his faith. Someone gave him Lewis's book *The Problem of Pain*, and Downing was astounded by the honesty with which Lewis opened that book. Lewis articulated the reality of what Downing was experiencing. The book began with a strong statement of the conviction Lewis once held: if there was a spirit behind the universe, it was an evil spirit.

It's easy to buy into a kind of dream-world faith in which God is explained, questions are answered, and pain is denied. But it's dangerous, because no one can explain God, some questions simply don't have answers, and a life without pain is impossible.

Consider Lewis's words, spoken in a time of war:

[War] makes death real to us: and that would have been regarded as one of its blessings by most of the great Christians of the past. They thought it good for us to be always aware of our mortality. I am inclined to think they were right. All the animal life in us, all schemes of happiness that centered in this world, were always doomed to a final frustration. In ordinary times only a wise [person] can realize it. Now the stupidest of us knows. We see unmistakably the sort of universe in which we have all along been living, and must come to terms with it. If we had foolish un-Christian hopes about human culture, they are now shattered. If we thought we were building up a heaven on earth, if we looked for something that would turn the present world from a place of pilgrimage into a permanent city satisfying the soul . . . we are disillusioned, and not a moment too soon. But if we thought that for some souls, and at some times, the life of learning, humbly offered to God, was, in its own small way, one of the appointed approaches to the Divine reality and the Divine beauty which we hope to enjoy hereafter, we can think so still.[1]

A number of years ago I wrote a book titled *When Your Rope Breaks*. That book has been translated into several languages, and I still hear from people who say they were helped by it. I'm glad. The book was written for those who are going through hard times, and I stand by everything I wrote. Theologically and biblically, it was accurate and correct. In fact, it wasn't half bad.

The only problem is that the author was too young to even know that the truth he wrote was true. Now I know that what I wrote so many years ago is still true. There are, however, a number of additions that I would make to that book if I had the opportunity.

I have a friend who was in a car accident nearly forty years ago. As she pulled out of a parking space, another vehicle plowed into the side of her car. Even after all these years, my friend says she sometimes braces herself when she pulls out of a parking space.

If you're into looking away from hard places of truth, you might want to skip over what follows. This is not going to be pretty. If you stay with me, I promise it will get better. Before we see the light, however, it's important to recognize the dark.

Over the years, since I wrote the book on broken ropes, I've noticed that I brace myself far more often than I did back then. Bracing oneself is the curse of experience.

THE WORLD IS ATTRACTIVE

I have to brace myself, because the world is far more attractive than I thought it was.

That truth may seem strange given what I wrote above. It seems a little strange to me too. I'm sort of like the man who wrote to the magazine subscription department: "When I subscribed a year ago, you stated that if I was not satisfied at the end of the year, I could have my money back. Well, I would like to have it back. On second thought, to save you the trouble, you may apply it to my next year's subscription."

Why would I be attracted to a dangerous world in which there is so much pain?

1. *I'm Attracted to the World because It's a Good Place to Sin*

The apostle John said that "what we will be has not yet appeared; but we know that when he appears we shall be like him" (1 John 3:2). That thrills me! That means the time is coming when I'm going to be like Jesus. I won't struggle with sin anymore; I won't have to deal with my addictions; I won't have to face temptation. That is so good.

I don't like admitting this, though: part of me is quite anxious about heaven. The Gatlin Brothers used to sing a song about a wino choir: if there was no Mogen David (wine) in heaven, they didn't want to go. I smile at that, but I do understand. Alcohol isn't my problem, but I have some others I'm not ready to leave behind. If I can't be angry in heaven, I'm not sure I want to go. If I can't lust, gossip, or feel self-righteous in heaven, I'm not sure I want to go. If I can't get the praises of people in heaven and it all goes to God instead, I'm not sure I want to go. If I can't be the center of attention in heaven, I'm not sure I want to go.

2. I'm Attracted to the World because of My Stuff

Paul wrote to Timothy, "Those who desire to be rich fall into temptation, into a snare, into many senseless and harmful desires that plunge people into ruin and destruction. For the love of money is a root of all kinds of evils. It is through this craving that some have wandered away from the faith and pierced themselves with many pangs" (1 Timothy 6:9–10).

Money may not be your sin or addiction, but substitute yours for money in that text. Whatever you're attracted to more than Christ is dangerous.

It is said that John Wesley once was being led around a rich man's estate. The man showed Wesley the magnificent formal gardens that surrounded the estate, the stables, and the large mansion with its expensive furnishings and works of art. Wesley reportedly said, "Ah, these are the things that make it hard for a man to die."

Comfort, sex, alcohol, drugs, religion, self-aggrandizement, someone you worship, a theological position you hold, or almost anything else that attracts you more than Christ is dangerous. It makes it hard to die.

The Jesus Movement of the sixties and seventies was a genuine spiritual awakening in America not altogether different from that of the Great Awakening in the eighteenth century. In the Jesus Movement, the lives of hundreds of thousands of young people were transformed, and we reap its benefits to this day.

At that time I was the pastor of a very formal and established

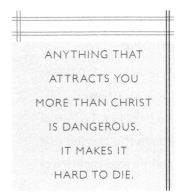

ANYTHING THAT
ATTRACTS YOU
MORE THAN CHRIST
IS DANGEROUS.
IT MAKES IT
HARD TO DIE.

Presbyterian church near Boston. When those freshly converted young people came into our church, everything changed—and it changed for the better. Our Sunday school grew, the congregation almost doubled, and we experienced a new life and vitality I've rarely seen in my ministry since.

I remember those young people, and even now I think of them with fondness—one young man in particular. Jamie had a ponytail, always wore jeans, and had a smile that would light up the world. He stayed in our church for a couple of years, teaching in the Sunday school, working in evangelism, and serving in any way he could. Then he decided to leave.

"Jamie," I said, "don't leave yet. I need you around here."

Jamie explained that he felt called to Colorado and that God had a place for him there. Nothing I could say would dissuade him from leaving. I can close my eyes even now and see Jamie walking down the hill from the church with his backpack over his shoulders. I had hugged him and promised to pray for him. I'll never forget what he said.

"You'd like to leave too, wouldn't you?"

I allowed that I was a bit envious.

"But Steve, you can't leave because you can't get everything you have in a backpack. When you can do that, you'll be free."

That was more profound than even he knew. When I can get it all—my reputation, my stuff, my needs, my dreams, my heart—in my backpack, then I'll be free. It doesn't all fit there now, and that's the reason I'm attracted to the world.

I'm getting better. Jesus is still fond of me, and he's helping me deal with my attachments. But I'm not there yet, and sometimes the world is quite attractive because of those attachments.

3. *I'm Attracted to the World because Dying Isn't an Altogether Happy Thought for Me*

I know, I know. Jesus said that anyone who believed in him would never die (John 11:26). After his death, Jesus got up from a grave—and he said I could do that too. That gives me great hope, and I'm grateful for his promise.

Still, something in me rebels against my own death. While that something may be from God, telling me I wasn't created for death, it still gets to me. When I was younger, I thought death happened to other people, or at least that science would find a cure for death before I got there. I'm a lot older now, and having seen the deaths of so many I love, I've been faced with the awesome and fearful reality that the statistic is one out of one. I'm really not going to get out of this thing alive. That makes me want to cling to the world for dear life. And that's dangerous.

The World Is Not Fair

I have to brace myself because the world isn't nearly as fair as I thought it was.

The world makes promises that are hard to ignore. Those promises don't sound like the "world" because they're often laced with "God words." But even though they sound religious, they aren't from him. The promises are from those who simply don't know what the Bible says. They say that if you're good, believe and trust in God, and read the Bible and pray, you have nothing to fear. When I was younger, I believed that. I might not have put it quite that way, but essentially, that was a basic philosophy in my life. What was I thinking?

I stopped believing in that when my brother died, my pastor got a divorce, my best friend—the godliest man I knew—was killed in an automobile accident, and a hurricane destroyed my house.

Jesus never lied to me, but the world did. Jesus said, "In the world you will have tribulation" (John 16:33). The world said I could be healthy, wealthy, and wise if I just exercised the right principles, was a good person, and put my faith in God. That's a lie. Oh, the people saying it didn't mean to lie. They wanted it to be true, they really believed it was true, and they taught that it was true. I did too. But it's still not true.

This is what is true: every day the world rolls over on top of a Christian who was just sitting on top of it. As I write this, a woman in our church choir is dying of cancer. They say she won't make it through the day. She sang in our worship team, she loved God, and we prayed for her. We prayed hard. But she's still dying, and that bothers me.

The world is a dangerous place because it isn't fair. It isn't fair to your unbelieving friends, and it isn't fair for Christians either. As attractive as they are, the promises simply aren't true, and you have to brace yourself against that reality.

There are, of course, promises the world makes that aren't particular to believers. There's the promise of pornography, the promise of wealth, the promise of addictions, the promise of another spouse who better fits your needs, the promise of education, the promise of fame, the promise of health from a gym or a vitamin, the promise of political power. There isn't enough room here to deal with each of these, but all of them promise to deliver very attractive paybacks.

Those are lies too.

THE WORLD IS NOT SAFE

I have to brace myself because the world isn't as safe as I thought it was.

I referred to this fact above, but let's get a bit more specific. We live in a culture that is obsessed with safety. I recently read a report that gave an astonishing statistic about the number of people who die from eating improper foods. The person relating the statistic seemed to suggest that if you eat properly, you won't die. What was that person thinking? Whether or not we eat properly, we're going to die.

I lived in the perfect neighborhood once. We loved it. The whole development had a white picket fence around it, the homes were all "country," and there was a clubhouse with a pool and all kinds of recreational amenities. A lake in our community gave people a nice place to fish and sail. The telephone and electrical wiring was underground so the beauty of our community wouldn't be marred by the ugliness of utility poles. Our neighbors were nice, our roads were clean and lined with big trees, and our houses and yards were well maintained. The police regularly patrolled our community, and we always felt safe. And the climate was just about perfect. My wife and I often took evening walks, thankful that we lived in that kind of community.

Then a hurricane blew through, and the entire community looked as though someone mowed it down with a gigantic lawnmower—houses, picket fences, clubhouse, trees, and all. Not a single two-story house remained a two-story house. Many of the one-story houses were totally destroyed, and not a single home remained intact.

After my first automobile accident, I found out that the roads weren't as safe as I thought they were. After my brother died, I found out that life wasn't as safe as I thought it was. After my first hurricane, I discovered that the world wasn't as safe as I thought it was either.

Someone sent me a story for my birthday. Let me share it with you:

Once upon a time, in the land of fuzzle-wuzzle, there lived a merry band of teddy bears. All day long they'd laugh and frolic in the fields and valleys. Every evening they'd sit down to a big banquet of honey muffins and oatmeal. After singing a round of silly songs, they'd get all comfy and cozy and fall asleep beneath the magical lollipop tree. This went on for years and years. . . .

. . . then the battle of Armageddon broke out and they all died. The end.

Hey, do I look like Mother Goose? Deal with it!

Happy Birthday!

No matter what we do to try to protect ourselves and those we love, or the things we love; however effective those efforts are—or are not—it's clear that the world is not a safe place. The question for us is, how will we deal with it?

Perhaps the answer is in how we think about the world. Which brings me to my final point.

THE WORLD IS NOT GOING TO LAST

I have to brace myself because the world isn't going to last the way I thought it would.

The Bible says, "The present form of this world is passing away" (1 Corinthians 7:31). Nothing we can feel, touch, or see right now is going to last. We can dance, rearrange the furniture, enjoy the meals, have parties, and celebrate; but if we're doing it on the *Titanic*, it's all simply an illusion of permanence.

The problem is that there is a conspiracy in which we all participate. We talk as if nothing will change. We build houses and churches, create monuments, establish institutions, and produce wealth . . . all in order to maintain the illusion that all of it, and we ourselves, are permanent. We embalm and dress up the corpse, but it's still a corpse. We paint over and repair our crumbling buildings, but even with our maintenance, in time they will crumble.

Plastic surgery, hair transplants, liposuction, cosmetics, brushed and enhanced photographs, energy pills, and vitamins are all a part of this conspiracy to make us think this all will last. Nothing will. Nothing is permanent.

Jesus told a story about a successful farmer who was hardworking and frugal. He was so successful that he had to tear down his barns and build bigger ones. The farmer sat on his front porch, looking over all that he created, and said to himself, "'You have ample goods laid up for many years; relax, eat, drink, be merry.'

"But God said to him, 'Fool! This night your soul is required of you, and the things you have prepared, whose will they be?'" (Luke 12:19–20).

That is a good question. Whose will they be? Maybe the farmer's goods would be passed along to his children and, when they died, to their children. Eventually, though, those things would be nobody's. Eventually, the Bible says, all those things will fade away into nothingness.

> THOSE WHO SAY JESUS IS ALL THEY NEED NEVER KNOW THAT JESUS IS ALL THEY NEED UNTIL JESUS IS ALL THEY'VE GOT.

I hate change. I hate any kind of change. When I was younger, I could maintain the illusion that things would be permanent. As I grow older, it's not so easy. Someone has said that you know you're getting old when you get down on the floor to retrieve something and ask yourself, *Is there anything else I can do while I'm down here?* Or, you know you're getting old when a pretty girl passes by and your pacemaker opens the garage door. Or, you know you're getting old when hardly anything in your body works, and what does work hurts.

Our humor is often truer than our philosophies. We work hard to maintain the illusion of permanence . . . but our nervous laughter betrays the truth. We know. We try to ignore it, to cover it, and to pretend . . . but we know. Nothing lasts.

That's bad.

No, actually, that's good. If you're still with me after all this doom and gloom, let me give you some good news. If what I've written in this chapter is true (and it is), then why do you care? Even more to the point, why do you believe, and why do you hope? One would think that the facts—once stated and faced—would lead to nothing but hopelessness, meaninglessness, and unbelief. "For men must work, and women must weep, And the sooner it's over, the sooner to sleep."[2]

I don't want this to be just another pious religious cliché, but the older I get, the more real Jesus has become and the less real, or even important, this dangerous world is. Someone has said that those who say Jesus is all they need never know that Jesus is all they need until Jesus is all they've got. When Jesus is all they've got, then they know that Jesus is all they need.

When I find that the world is far more dangerous than I thought it was, something in me says that it isn't supposed to be that way. Something in my genes says that there is a paradise that has been lost, a security that has been shattered, and a reality that is missing. A dangerous and fleeting world makes me look beyond it.

The understanding that the world is dangerous comes with age, with sin, with fear, and with shattered dreams. With all of that, however, comes also a yearning for something more. If this world were less dangerous, less fleeting, and more secure, I may never have found the only place that is more secure than the world is dangerous.

I just saw a picture of a man wearing a T-shirt that read, "I'm a bomb technician. If you see me running, try to keep up." In other words, a bomb is getting ready to explode, I can't fix it, and I'm running as fast as I can to get away from it. So keep up.

In this world there's only one safe place to run. I told you earlier what Jesus said about tribulation: that in the world—a dangerous world—we will have tribulation. That's a cold, hard fact. Deal with it.

But that wasn't all he said.

What else did Jesus say?

"I have said these things to you, that in me you may have peace. In the world you will have tribulation. But take heart; I have overcome the world" (John 16:33).

The "bomb" has exploded.

But I know where to run.

SOMETIMES PROVIDENCES, LIKE HEBREW
LETTERS, MUST BE READ BACKWARD.

JOHN FLAVEL

THINGS WILL WORK OUT A LOT BETTER THAN I THOUGHT THEY WOULD

*We know that for those who love God
all things work together for good.*

ROMANS 8:28

WE WON!

Well, that's rather crass. It wasn't really a matter of winning and losing. However, when American ecclesiastical history is written about the twentieth and early twenty-first centuries, one of the great surprises will be the resurgence of evangelicalism. I'm an evangelical, and it did feel like we won.

No one would have expected it.

When I decided to become an evangelical, it wasn't a very popular thing to do.[1] In fact, it was ecclesiastical suicide. My friends thought I had lost my mind, and those who weren't friends said they always knew something was wrong with me. I can remember the pastor of a prominent church in the city where I ministered crossing over to the other side of the street so he wouldn't have to speak to me.

I'm thankful that I made the decision when it wasn't popular. Knowing me, my motivations would have been less pure if I had waited until we "won." When I decided to become an evangelical, almost all of our churches were small, our seminaries were considered second-rate, and our books and magazines were only read by a small group of "Bible thumpers" who were, as a prominent reporter said, "uneducated and easily led."

I graduated from a mainline "liberal" graduate school of theology, where the words *evangelical* and *scholar* could not be used in the same sentence. In those days we considered evangelicals obscurant, shallow, and unsophisticated.

When *Christianity Today*—a magazine designed to stand for orthodox theology—was founded by Billy Graham and a number of other well-known evangelicals, it was distributed free to pastors and theology students. I remember bound stacks of those magazines left in the seminary lobby. They were never opened and never read. We, of course, read *Christian Century*, the liberal magazine of note, and we sometimes made fun of that "other" magazine.

My decision to become an evangelical was a matter of conscience and need. I was then serving as the student pastor of a small church on Cape Cod. It had become quite apparent that I didn't have much to say of any worth or at least anything that made much difference to people who were sinners—afraid, wounded, and empty. To this day I don't understand how a theological liberal can be a pastor. If you don't believe the doctrines of Scripture, why would you want to be a pastor? That seems insane to me. Anyway, at that time I was, in fact, thinking about leaving.

It's a long story, and the details aren't relevant here, but my move toward evangelicalism involved God's miraculous intervention in my life through the healing of our daughter, some evangelical friends who were intellectuals, and some dear people who loved me and prayed for me.

Bottom line, I joined the "other side."

When I joined the evangelical wing of the church, I knew that I probably would never serve a big church, write books anyone would ever read, or be accepted or liked by those who "mattered" in the American church in general and my denomination in particular. But it didn't matter. Jesus still loved me, and that was enough. He had forgiven, accepted, and called me, and I didn't care where we went or what we did as long as he went with me.

Then a funny thing happened on the way to ecclesiastical oblivion. We won!

To this day I'm not sure what happened. (A number of books have been written on the phenomenal evangelical growth.[2]) Some of it had to do with the Jesus Movement, some of it happened because of the media, and some of it happened because people grew tired of religious platitudes and shallow unbelief cloaked in "God words." But when the history of evangelicalism is written, it will include a great number of faithful Christians who kept "the faith that was once for all delivered to the saints" (Jude 1:3) through some lean years of scorn, rejection, and dismissal.

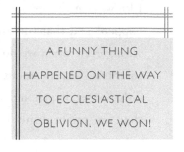

A FUNNY THING HAPPENED ON THE WAY TO ECCLESIASTICAL OBLIVION. WE WON!

I woke up one day to find that evangelical colleges, seminaries, and churches were showing explosive growth. Evangelical books were becoming bestsellers, and *Christianity Today* was the most successful magazine in the history of Christianity. I heard about John Lennon, Bob Dylan, Keith Richards, and Bono announcing they had become Christians.

And all of a sudden I found myself on the "winning side" of the ecclesiastical battle.

I'm not even sure that "winning" was a good thing for the church, but I do know that it was a good thing for me. It meant that what I thought would be a harmful career decision so many years ago, in fact, turned out to be a smart move. I preach in mega-churches, I write books that people read, I have a successful media ministry, and I teach at a prominent seminary—one of the largest in the world. None of that should have happened. For a number of reasons, things really did work out a lot better than I thought they would.

They generally do for believers. No, I haven't lost my mind. I know that things don't always work out well. I know that stuff happens and that this isn't a safe world. I know things often go wrong even when we do right, and some problems have no good solutions. I know about cancer, accidents, and Down syndrome kids. Generally, though, for believers, things do work out better than one might think. Let's look at a few reasons why.

TRUTH

Things work out better because of truth.

Jesus said, "If you abide in my word, you are truly my disciples, and you will know the truth, and the truth will set you free" (John 8:31–32). Paul wrote, "Stand therefore, having fastened on the belt of truth" (Ephesians 6:14). John wrote of Christ's coming that, while Moses brought the Law, "truth came through Jesus Christ" (John 1:17).

Have you noticed some of the silly things some people believe? Some believe that if you get a crystal, join a lot of people on a mountaintop in Arizona, hold hands, and sound out together, "*Ohmmmmm*," you'll end world hunger and bring world peace. Others believe that human nature is basically good, so they don't lock their doors. Some think it doesn't matter what you believe as long as you believe something and are sincere about it. I know people who believe you can cure cancer with a spoonful of honey and others who think the world owes them and live their lives as victims. There are even people who call good evil and evil good and who think it doesn't matter what you do as long as you don't hurt anybody.

I'm not that dumb. Well, maybe I am, but God has graciously revealed the truth to me, and it is surprising how often I appear smart and things seem to work out better than I thought they would . . . simply because I know that truth.

I have a friend who, before every important, right, and controversial decision I've made over the last twenty-five years, said to me, "Steve, if you do right, it will come out right." He is, I think, looking at the long view and making the point that ultimately no good deed, no wise decision, and no right action will be lost. He's talking about a God who is sovereign over everything and who will ultimately balance all the books and settle all the accounts.

I understand that, but I also believe things will "come out right" before they come out right in the end. I believe that you usually do receive what you give, that you'll be judged by the same judgment with which you judge others, and that bread cast on waters really does come back to you. I believe that if you exalt yourself, generally you will be humbled, and if you humble yourself, generally you will be exalted. I think that if you do to others what you would have them do to you—if you go the second mile and are kind—there is a great payback in this life.

Some Christians believe they're called to go through hell in order to get to heaven. They also think unbelievers go through heaven in order to get to hell. In other words, they think things are really hard for them now, but later they will have a dynamite "retirement"—and that those of you who don't believe will have a good time now, but "you'll get yours" one of these days.

That is neurotic. Of course there are hard things about following Christ, and there really is a heaven. But could it be, do you think, that maybe a Christian, because he or she knows the truth, will get a bit of heaven before going there?

If you're reading this book and you aren't a Christian, let me give you some good advice. If you want to be happier, to have things go better, and to be more at peace than you are now, read the Bible and do what it says as best you can. That won't be easy because some of it won't make sense to you, and you may not have a lot of help. But if you're disciplined enough and stay with it, you'll be able to do some of it.

You say, "But I don't believe the Bible." That's OK; I'm not your mother. Just as an experiment, do what I've suggested. You'll be surprised at how much better things work out.

LOVE

Things also work out better because of love.

Jesus said, "As the Father has loved me, so have I loved you. Abide in my love" (John 15:9). Paul said it's the love of Christ that controls us (see 2 Corinthians 5:14) and that nothing will ever be able to separate us from the love of Christ (see Romans 8:38–39).

I already spent time on this subject, and I don't want to overdo it, but I'm always surprised by God's love for me. It's his default position. I'd like to give you a list of my lovable qualities, the ones that attract God to me, but I can't think of any. There really is something unreasonable about God's love for his children.

The man or woman who isn't surprised by the love of God has never experienced the love of God and has no idea how little he or she deserves it. Christ really did die for the ungodly.

> THE MAN OR WOMAN WHO ISN'T SURPRISED BY THE LOVE OF GOD HAS NEVER EXPERIENCED THE LOVE OF GOD AND HAS NO IDEA HOW LITTLE HE OR SHE DESERVES IT.

I don't know about you, but I'm attracted to people who like me. I hate to admit that, but it's true. God's love does not discriminate, and mine does. I get thousands of letters in my line of work, and many of them are critical and angry, but I get a number of affirming and encouraging ones too. I answer both kinds, but the ones that affirm me receive longer, kinder, more loving answers, because I'm attracted to people who like me.

Jesus likes me big time, and my default position is to run to him. I always think he'll be angry, tell me he's had it with me, and tell me to become a Buddhist instead. But that has never happened. And it's always surprising.

Our family has always had German shepherds. Thor is the fifth shepherd in our family. The other four are now in heaven, and if you don't believe that dogs go to heaven, keep your spurious theological views to yourself.

I really do love Thor, but I still haven't gotten over the death of our last shepherd, Quincy the Wonder Dog. I guess I loved him because, when he was a puppy, they were going to put him down because of his bad hips. The breeder from whom we bought Quincy said she would give us our money back but that it was unconscionable for him to be allowed to breed. So, with the promise that he would be "fixed," we let Quincy live. I guess you could say I saved his life.

To alleviate the hip problem, our veterinarian said Quincy's hips could be removed, and cartilage would grow in their place. He said Quincy would be "almost normal," and he was almost normal for twelve years. The procedure to make Quincy almost normal was extremely painful, and I remember picking him up at the vet's office after the surgery. I had to carry him to the car, and my every movement elicited a whimper from Quincy.

I took him to our family room and laid him on a blanket in the corner. I was sure Quincy would never want anything to do with me again, given that I was the one who had taken him to the vet and thus was responsible for all of his pain. If I could win back Quincy's trust, I was sure it would take a long time.

I sat down in my easy chair and started reading the paper. After about five minutes, I felt something move the paper. I looked down, and it was Quincy. He laid his head on my lap.

I prayed, "Oh God, let me be that way with you. There is so much pain, but let me always come to you and put my head on your lap the way Quincy has just done with me."

One more story about Quincy. (If you aren't a "dog person," you probably just want me to move on, but if you know and love dogs, you'll like this story.)

It was many years later when our vet informed us that Quincy wouldn't live much longer. We took Quincy home from that appointment, and I was out in the backyard playing with him. Quincy loved chasing and retrieving anything I threw—a Frisbee, a stick, or a ball. So I threw a stick, and as best as he could, Quincy ran to retrieve it. Just as he picked it up, his back went out for the final time. Do you know what he did? He pulled himself with his front elbows across the yard to bring the stick to me.

I prayed, "Oh, God, let me be that way with you."

Quincy loved being with me more than anything else. When I came home, he waited by the door to greet me. When I left, he stood by the door to watch me go. No matter what my mood, he just loved to be around me.

Now, as some of you may know, German shepherds can be pretty scary dogs. We locked the doors in our house to protect the thieves, not our stuff. Our German shepherds always protected our stuff and our family. If you'd met Quincy, you might have been a bit wary, because he was quite a large German shepherd. Quincy looked dangerous, but he wasn't dangerous at all. He was the most gentle and loving dog you would ever meet, and he would run to anybody just to have his ears scratched.

Quincy was a loved dog, and he became a loving dog. When you meet a mean dog, you can almost always assume it has a mean owner. A dog who is loved, however, is a loving dog.

Human beings are like that too. I've walked with God for so long, have run to him so much, and have been loved by him so deeply that I am a far more loving person than I would be if I had never known him. His love has become the defining factor in my life, and he has loved me into becoming a loving person. One can't love until one has been loved—and then only to the degree to which one has been loved. Jesus said there was no greater love than the love manifested when a man died for his friends.

Then he called me his friend.

I don't think God has called me to discipline, to condemn, or to judge people. I tell them the truth, but I'm not in the business of playing God. He told me to love, and insofar as I allow God to love me, I'm able to love others. The great thing about that is, when you love people, they love you back. They also help you, cover for you, and encourage you to be better. That's why things have worked out a lot better than I thought they would. It's because of love.

GRACE

Things work out better because of grace.

In the first chapter of John cited earlier, John said that the Law came through Moses and that, not only did truth come through Jesus, but grace came through him too (see John 1:17). Paul wrote, "But the free gift is not like the trespass. For if many died through one man's trespass [i.e., Adam's sin], much more have the grace of God and the free gift by the grace of that one man Jesus Christ abounded for many. . . . Where sin increased, grace abounded all the more" (Romans 5:15–20). He wrote in Ephesians 2:8–9, "By grace you have been saved through faith. And this is not your own doing; it is the gift of God, not a result of works, so that no one may boast."

My pastor, Pete Alwinson, has the best definition of grace: "Grace," he says, "is doing good for someone when there is no compelling reason to do so and every reason not to." That's it. That is what God has done and continues to do for me.

Art DeMoss, the founder of the Arthur S. DeMoss foundation, was an acquaintance of mine and one of the most effective evangelists I've ever known. A flight attendant friend of mine met him once on a flight. She told me, "I'm a Christian, but I had the feeling that if I had not already been one, I would have become one before the flight ended." Art loved Christ, he loved people, and he loved life.

Anyway, whenever someone asked Art how he was doing, he answered with his standard response: "I'm doing a lot better than I deserve." That's what grace does. Grace is a gift of a lot more than the recipient deserves.

Groucho Marx once said that he would never join a club that would have him as a member. I sort of feel that way about the church. It's insane, what I do. As I can't but help point out again, I—who ran away from kindergarten—now teach at a graduate school of theology. I struggle with sin as much as anybody I know, and yet I'm a preacher. I graduated fourth from the bottom of a large high school, yet you are now reading a book I wrote. I hate religion as much as anybody I know, and now I'm a religious professional. Not only that. I have enough money to pay the mortgage, and I have a beautiful wife and wonderful daughters and granddaughters. I drive, as I told you, a brand-new hybrid car, can afford to take my wife to dinner at almost any restaurant, and own the computer at which I am now typing.

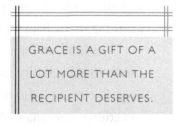

GRACE IS A GIFT OF A LOT MORE THAN THE RECIPIENT DESERVES.

Why is that? Is it because I'm smart, good, and wise? No.

God is gracious, and everything I am, do, and have is a gift of his grace. If I received his justice, I'd be dead.

Earlier on, I shared with you a partial quote from my friend Jack Miller. Now let me share with you all of what he said. Jack used to say that the whole Bible can be summed up in two statements: (1) Cheer up: you're a lot worse than you think you are. (2) Cheer up: God's grace is a lot bigger than you think it is.

Grace is the reason things work out a lot better than I thought they would. It's because things work out a lot better than I deserve.

Clout in High Places

Things work out better because I have clout in some very high places.

Let me share with you an amazing statement made by Jesus: "Truly, truly, I say to you, whoever believes in me will also do the works that I do; and greater works than these will he do, because I am going to the Father. Whatever you ask in my name, this I will do, that the Father may be glorified in the Son. If you ask me anything in my name, I will do it" (John 14:12–14).

That kind of statement makes us uncomfortable because it speaks to a possibility that doesn't often connect with our experience. But anyone who teaches that text in a way to make Jesus say something other than what he said is wrong.

From an understanding of the whole counsel of God, the Bible, it's obvious that Jesus was not giving us carte blanche to do spiritual magic tricks. But Jesus did tell us that we have a connection to God, enabling us to go to him with any need and any problem. Someone once asked G. Campbell Morgan, the great Bible teacher, if it was OK to go to God with little things. He answered, "Madam, do you know of anything that isn't little to God?"

As I mentioned, I've interviewed best-selling author Anne Lamott on a couple of occasions. While I don't agree with her politics or her theology, I don't think I've ever met anyone more authentic or who loves Jesus more. The first time I interviewed Anne, it was a phone interview taped from a Miami studio. She was late for an appointment, and it was obvious that she didn't want to be interviewed. Anne asked if I could keep it short. I told her that I would do that, but I needed to tell her something before we began.

"Anne," I asked, "do you know those fundamentalist types, the Bible thumpers, the ones who are often condemning?"

Anne said she did, and the way she said it gave me an indication that her experience had not been altogether that positive.

"Well," I confessed, "I'm one of them. But before you jump to conclusions, I want you to know that I loved your book, have given it to all my friends, and have probably sold more copies than you have."

(A smart move. Authors like people who like their books.)

That interview turned out to be a great one—in fact, it went on for some time. I actually had trouble bringing it to a close. Just before our conversation ended, this is what Anne said: "Steve, do you know what we would do if we ever met?"

"No, Anne," I said. "What would we do if we met?"

"We would hold hands and tell each other stories about Jesus."

Earlier I told you about Anne Lamott's three kinds of prayer: "God, help me right now!" "Wow!" and "Thank you, God." Well, there isn't a Christian reading this who can't identify with those words. We've all been in pits so deep that only God could get us out, in sin so bad that no one else would ever forgive, and in pain so heartbreaking that no doctor could fix. We have all called out to God, "Help me!" And we have all—not all the time, but sometimes—seen God do exactly what we asked. And we've said, "Wow!" and then thanked him.

That is why things will work out a lot better than I thought they would.

HEAVEN

Finally, things work out better because of heaven.

Jesus said, "I am the resurrection and the life. Whoever believes in me, though he die, yet shall he live, and everyone who lives and believes in me shall never die" (John 11:25–26). He promised the thief who died on the cross next to him, "Today you will be with me in Paradise" (Luke 23:43). Paul said that whether we live or die, we're the Lord's (see Romans 14:8). And when we were no longer in our bodies, we will be present before God (see 2 Corinthians 5:8).

In other words, even if things don't work out as well as we thought they would or should, the story isn't over. Things *will* work out fine. A missionary complained that no one cared, because when he came home from the mission field, nobody was there to meet him. "Son," God told him, "you aren't Home yet."

We aren't Home yet, you know. As an old guy beginning to "cram for finals," I've discovered that I really don't have to cram. It has all been done for me, and in the end, I'll be Home. The angels may blush, but they will sing, and I'll be welcomed.

The late Peter Marshall, chaplain to the U.S. Senate, said that when he died, he would stand before God, and all his sins would be read out. Then, just when God was ready to pronounce judgment, Jesus would put his hand on Marshall's shoulder and say, "It's all right, Father. I took care of Peter's sins on the cross." Then he would be welcomed Home.

During the time I've been writing this chapter, I received an e-mail informing me that the grandmother of one of our former employees, Dawn Givens, had died. It reminded me of the story Dawn told me years ago, when her grandfather died. He'd long been sick, and it had been a difficult time for the family.

> "IT'S ALL RIGHT, FATHER. I TOOK CARE OF PETER'S SINS ON THE CROSS."

Dawn's grandmother, of course, had been devastated by the loss. Some family members arranged to take turns staying with her during the long and lonely nights following her husband's death. One night her great-grandson Jay ("Jay Bird") stayed with her. He was a small boy then, perhaps three or four years old. For purposes of this story, you need to know that Jay called his great-grandmother "Me-Mommy" and his great-grandfather "Paw-Paw."

The night Jay Bird stayed with his great-grandmother, she said prayers with him and then tucked him into bed. "Me-Mommy," Jay said, "do you know what I'm going to do?"

"No, Jay Bird. What are you going to do?"

"I'm going to pray that God will let me dream about Paw-Paw tonight."

"That would be nice," she said, turning off the light.

Jay had only known his great-grandfather when the elderly man was sick. In fact, Jay had never seen his "Paw-Paw" not in a wheelchair.

The next morning Jay's great-grandmother came into his room to find Jay jumping up and down on his bed. She asked him why he was so happy. Jay said that he had dreamed of Paw-Paw. Jay said he had seen Paw-Paw walking and that he (Jay) had run up to him, and his great-grandfather picked him up and hugged him.

"How did he look?" she asked.

"Fine," he said.

"No, Jay," she said, "I mean, did he look sick?"

"No! He didn't look sick. He was new!"

At times I have despaired, doubting that all this—this messy, dangerous, up-and-down life—could ever end well. What was I thinking?

Things are going to work out a lot better than I thought they would.

We're going to be new!

NOTES

CHAPTER 2: JESUS IS A LOT MORE RADICAL THAN I THOUGHT HE WAS
1. Albert Schweitzer, *The Quest of the Historical Jesus*, ed. John Bowden (Mineapolis: Augsburg Fortress Press, 2001).

CHAPTER 3: THE HOLY SPIRIT IS WORKING IN A LOT MORE PLACES THAN I THOUGHT HE WAS
1. Steve Brown, *Follow the Wind* (Grand Rapids: Baker Books, 1999).
2. If you are interested in pursuing some of H. R. Rookmaaker's thoughts on this subject, let me suggest his book *The Creative Gift: Essays on Art and the Christian Life* (Crossway Book, 1981).
3. Henry P. Van Dusen, *Spirit, Son and Father* (New York: Charles Scribner's Sons, 1958), 25.
4. Reggie M. Kidd, *With One Voice: Discovering Christ's Song in Our Worship* (Grand Rapids: Baker Books, 2005).
5. William D. Romanowski, *Eyes Wide Open: Looking for God in Popular Culture* (Grand Rapids: Brazos Press, 2001), 13–14.
6. Leland Ryken, *The Liberated Imagination* (Wheaton, Ill.: Harold Shaw Publishers, 1989), 166.
7. Don Richardson, *Eternity in Their Hearts* (Ventura, Calif.: Regal Books, 1984).

CHAPTER 4: THE BIBLE REVEALS A LOT MORE THAN I THOUGHT IT DID
1. Émile Cailliet, *Journey into Light* (Grand Rapids: Zondervan Publishers, 1968).
2. Arthur Bennett, ed., *The Valley of Vision: A Collection of Puritan Prayers and Devotions* (Edinburgh: The Banner of Truth, 2002), 150–51.
3. Richard Pratt, *He Gave Us Stories* (Phillipsburg, N.J.: P & R Publishing, 1990).

CHAPTER 5: THE BATTLE IS A LOT MORE SUPERNATURAL THAN I THOUGHT IT WAS
1. John White, *The Fight* (Downers Grove, Ill.: InterVarsity Press, 1978), 12.
2. Anne Lamott, *Traveling Mercies: Some Thoughts on Faith* (New York: Pantheon Books, 1999).

CHAPTER 6: PEOPLE ARE A LOT WORSE THAN I THOUGHT THEY WERE
1. Deborah Layton, *Seductive Poison: A Jonestown Survivor's Story of Life and Death in the Peoples Temple* (New York: Anchor Books, 1999), 4–5.
2. Brennan Manning, *The Wisdom of Tenderness* (New York: HarperSanFrancisco, 2002), 62.

CHAPTER 7: People Are a Lot Better Than I Thought They Were

1. Richard Pratt, *Designed for Dignity: What God Has Made It Possible for You to Be* (Phillipsburg, N.J.: P & R Publishing, 1993), 50.

2. Spencer Lewerenz and Barbara Nicolosi, eds., *Behind the Screen: Hollywood Insiders on Faith, Film, and Culture* (Grand Rapids: Baker Books, 2005), 8–9.

CHAPTER 8: Self-Righteousness Is a Lot More Dangerous Than I Thought It Was

1. Calvin Miller, *The Singer Trilogy* (Downers Grove, Ill.: InterVasersity Press, 1975), 121.

CHAPTER 9: Obedience Is a Lot More Difficult Than I Thought It Was

1. Martin Luther, quoted by C. F. W. Walther in "The Proper Distinction Between Law and Gospel" (lecture, originally published by Concordia Publishing House, 1929, now in public domain), http://lutherantheology.com/walther/LG/index.html.

2. Martin Luther, quoted in CEP Online, http://cep.anglican.ca/community/viewtopic.php?t=371&highlight=&sid=7cf4a60ea9cd3de480212805d918d8f.

3. Donald Miller, *Blue Like Jazz: Nonreligious Thoughts on Christian Spirituality* (Nashville: Thomas Nelson Publishers, 2003).

CHAPTER 10: Love Is a Lot Stronger Than I Thought It Was

1. Stephen J. Nichols, *Martin Luther: A Guided Tour of His Lide and Thought* (Phillipsburg, N.J.: P & R Publishing, 2002), 50.

2. Ibid.

3. C. S. Lewis, *The Four Loves* (New York: Harvest Books, 1971).

CHAPTER 11: The World Is a Lot More Dangerous Than I Thought It Was

1. C. S. Lewis, "Learning in War-Time" (sermon, Oxford, 1939).

2. Charles Kingsley, "The Three Fishers," Representative Poetry Online, University of Toronto, http://rpo.library.utoronto.ca/poem/1164.html.

CHAPTER 12: Things Will Work Out a Lot Better Than I Thought They Would

1. *Evangelical* is from a Latin word taken from Greek. It means "good news." As I use it here, I mean those who have a conservative/orthodox theology. Evangelicals accept the full authority of the Bible and center on the doctrine of salvation by faith in Christ alone. Evangelicals take a varietey of theological positions. My particular view is called Reformed, referring to the doctrines of the Protestant Reformation.

2. For example, Dean Kelley's book *Why Conservative Churches Are Growing* (New York: Harper & Row, 1972) and David Shiflett's book *Exodus: Why Americans Are Fleeing Liberal Churches for Conservative Christianity* (New York: Sentinel Publishers, 2005).

Printed in the United States
By Bookmasters